CIVIL WAR SPRINGFIELD

Civil War Springfield

Larry Wood

Series Editor Doug Bostick

The History Press

Published by The History Press
Charleston, SC 29403
www.historypress.net

Cover image: *That Beautiful Charge*, Andy Thomas, artist, Carthage, Missouri.

First published 2011

Manufactured in the United States

ISBN 978.1.60949.308.0

Wood, Larry (Larry E.)
Civil War Springfield / Larry Wood ; series editor, Doug Bostick.
p. cm.
Includes bibliographical references and index.
ISBN 978-1-60949-308-0
1. Springfield (Mo.)--History, Military--19th century. 2. Springfield Region (Mo.)--History, Military--19th century. 3. Battles--Missouri--Springfield--History--19th century. 4. Battles--Missouri--Springfield Region--History--19th century. 5. Missouri--History--Civil War, 1861-1865--Campaigns. 6. Missouri--Military relations--Kansas. 7. Kansas--Military relations--Missouri. 8. United States--History--Civil War, 1861-1865--Campaigns. I. Bostick, Douglas W. II. Title.
F474.S7W66 2011
977.8'7803--dc23
2011041390

Contents

Acknowledgements

A writer of history usually needs considerable help from other people because completing a work of history involves tasks like doing research and gathering images in addition to the actual writing. I know that I received a lot of help in completing this book, and I would like to thank those individuals who facilitated the task for me.

As usual, the Joplin Public Library was the starting point of my research and the facility through which I obtained many materials via interlibrary loan. I would particularly like to thank the reference staff at the Joplin Public Library, including Patty Crane, Jason Sullivan, Jill Halbach-Boswell, Cheryl Smith, and Chris Hamm.

Many of the images in the book came from the Wilson's Creek Civil War Museum at the Wilson's Creek National Battlefield, and I want to thank the museum and its staff, particularly Deborah Wood and Alan Chilton, for making the images available to me. I also spent time researching at the Hulston Library at Wilson's Creek, and I want to thank librarian Jeff Patrick and his volunteer staff for their help.

Joan Hampton-Porter, curator of the Springfield–Greene County Historical Museum, was very helpful during my research visit to the museum. Joan and the museum also provided a couple of images that I have used in the book.

I made several trips to the Springfield–Greene County Library Center to research in the Local History section, and I would like to thank the library staff, particularly Patti Hobbs and Michael Glenn, for their help during those visits.

Robert Neumann and his staff also provided helpful assistance during a couple of visits I made to the Greene County Archives and Records Center.

I need to mention the staff at the Missouri State Archives in Jefferson City and the staff at the State Historical Society of Missouri in Columbia, both of which I found helpful during my visits, although I neglected to collect individual names.

I want to say a special thanks to Andy and Dina Thomas for allowing me to use an image of one of Andy's paintings on the cover of the book.

J. Dale West has provided me with several images for past projects, and he again allowed me to use an image from his collection for this book.

My wife, Gigi, served as the first reader of the manuscript, and I thank her for both her proofreading skills and her support.

Lastly, I want to say thanks to History Press project editor Ryan Finn for his thorough and competent review of the manuscript. I know that his contribution has enhanced the overall quality of the final product.

Introduction

In 1830, John Polk Campbell brought his family to southwest Missouri from Tennessee and settled near a spring, where he had staked a claim the previous year in an area that later became Springfield. The site is located near the present-day Founders Park at the corner of Jefferson and Water Streets. In 1835, Campbell laid out the town of Springfield and donated a fifty-acre tract of land to the new village. The same year, Springfield was named the county seat of Greene County, which had been formed two years earlier. In 1837, a courthouse was built on the public square, and the next year the town was officially incorporated.

By the eve of the Civil War, Springfield boasted a population of about 1,200 residents. Some estimates place the figure higher than this, but the 1860 census reveals that Campbell Township as a whole, encompassing not only Springfield but also the rural areas surrounding the town, had a white population of only 2,616. So the 1,200 figure for Springfield proper is probably accurate. However, because it was the principal town in the still-frontier region of southwest Missouri, Springfield was more important than its size might have indicated.

As the editor of the *Springfield Mirror* said in 1859, even though the town was a small place, the residents were "by no means an idle people." At the time, according to the newspaperman, Springfield had sixteen mercantile stores, two drugstores, two tobacconists, ten carpenters, seven blacksmith shops, two tinsmiths, two saddle and harness makers, three wagon and buggy shops, three taverns, three jewelers, and two printing offices. In addition, the town boasted three churches, five schools, ten lawyers, several doctors, and several fraternal organizations. The main thing wanting in Springfield, according to the editor, was a railroad. Once a railroad line reached the town, he predicted, Springfield would prosper greatly.

Even without a railroad, Springfield, as the center of commerce for southwest Missouri, was considered a strategic location by both sides during the Civil War. From the beginning of the war, the town functioned as a supply depot and gathering place for armies, and it served as a military headquarters for much of the conflict. North and South vied throughout the war to see which side would occupy Springfield, and control of the town seesawed back and forth early on.

Springfield bustled with activity, and sometimes the action got warm, such as during the Battle of Wilson's Creek, when the town served as a hospital for the wounded, and during the Battle of Springfield, when many locals took part in the defense of their own town. This book, however, is not just about battles. It is a book about Springfield as it was during the Civil War.

Chapter 1

The Prewar Years

Kansas Bleeds into Southwest Missouri

The bombardment of Fort Sumter by Confederate artillery in April 1861 marked the official beginning of the Civil War, but it is scarcely a stretch to suggest that the war actually began several years earlier on the Kansas-Missouri border during the battle over Kansas statehood that came to be known as "Bleeding Kansas." In fact, the roots of the Civil War can be traced even further back, at least to the birth of the nation, when sectional disagreement over the issue of slavery led to the adoption of the "three-fifths" compromise in the United States Constitution. The slavery issue was still festering in 1820 when the Missouri Compromise stipulated that Missouri would be admitted to the Union as a slave state (while Maine was admitted as a free state) but that no additional states lying north of Missouri's southern border could be admitted as slave states. The Kansas-Nebraska Act of 1854, however, effectively nullified the Missouri Compromise by opening those two new territories to white settlement and stipulating that, in the name of "popular sovereignty," the people residing in the territories would decide for themselves whether they wanted to allow slavery within their boundaries.

Nebraska, by virtue of its more northerly location, was destined from the beginning to be a free territory, and the question of slavery was never in doubt there. However, the Kansas-Nebraska Act ushered in a period of strife and violence in Kansas that presaged the Civil War. Already surrounded on the north and east by the free states of Iowa and Illinois, the slaveholders of Missouri felt threatened by the prospect of a free state to their west that

In eastern Kansas, rabid abolitionists like John Brown clashed with "Border Ruffians" during the prewar years. *From* Frank Leslie's Weekly, *courtesy of Library of Congress.*

would form the third link in an encircling chain of free-soil territory. A free Kansas might serve as a haven for stolen and runaway slaves and spell doom for the slaveholding interests of wealthy Missourians. In response to the threat, prominent landowners organized squads of men during the mid- to late 1850s to trek to Kansas to vote illegally in territorial elections on the proslavery side and to otherwise oppose the free-soil settlers who had begun flooding into Kansas from the Northern and New England states. Earning the name "Border Ruffians," the Missourians, in their zeal and devotion to their cause, sometimes resorted to violence, as did rabid abolitionists like John Brown on the free-soil side.

Most early residents of the Missouri Ozarks were poor hill folk who had come from the upper tier of Southern states, especially the Appalachian region of those states. The vast majority did not own slaves, and their economic interests lay increasingly with the North. However, they were tied to the South by bonds of kinship and culture, and they tended to support the wealthy landowners and slaveholders who dominated Missouri politics. Thus, the people of Springfield and Greene County, according to Holcombe's 1883 history of the county, "took a more or less conspicuous part…upon the pro-slavery side" in the Bleeding Kansas conflict. In addition to sending its fair share of Border Ruffians to stuff the Kansas ballot boxes, Greene County was also home to a secret proslavery organization akin to the Knights of the Golden Circle. The clandestine society maintained three or four lodges in different locations throughout the county, and members of the cloak-and-dagger outfit hailed one another with esoteric signs, grips, and passwords.

In July 1856, about a dozen men from Greene County joined a proslavery party from southwest Missouri for a journey to Kansas to fight the abolitionists, but when they reached the border, they found that recent hostilities in the region had already ceased and that their services were not needed. In August of the same year, "Judge" R.G. Roberts of Fort Scott, Kansas, spoke at Springfield in support of the proslavery cause and stirred up the like-minded men of Greene County. Shortly afterward, on September 1, the proslavery men of the county congregated for a mass meeting at the courthouse on the Springfield square. Several prominent citizens gave stirring speeches denouncing abolitionism, and the gathering adopted resolutions condemning the free-soil movement and pledging support for the proslavery people of Kansas. A number of men in the crowd enrolled as "minutemen," pledging themselves to go to Kansas at a moment's notice to fight the abolitionists, and a large sum of money was raised in support of the proslavery cause in Kansas.

The proslavery fervor that characterized southwest Missouri and Greene County during the Bleeding Kansas years, however, did not translate into secessionist sentiment as the Civil War approached. Although proslavery feelings in the region were widespread, the sentiment against disunion was even stronger. The proceedings of a series of meetings held in Springfield during the spring of 1858 illustrate the strength of this middle-of-the-road sentiment in the Greene County area.

Springfield was a small, rural town at the beginning of the Civil War. *Sketch from* Harper's Weekly *by Alexander Simplot.*

A large group of citizens, with Greene County probate judge Sample Orr presiding, met on April 5 with the idea of establishing a "Union Party," the only rallying cry or motto of which would be the preservation of the "Federal Union." The group stated its belief, according to the *Jefferson City Inquirer*, that "the tendency of what is termed National Democracy is the same as that which is termed Black Republicanism, both parties aiming at a dissolution of the Union, and therefore unworthy of trust." The meeting adopted a resolution condemning attempts in either the North or the South to establish two parties, antagonistic toward each other and sectional in nature that, should these efforts be consummated, would "most surely end disastrously to this government, by destroying the bonds of Union." The gathering also adopted a resolution condemning the Kansas-Nebraska Act as having produced "evils, civil war, bloodshed, murders, robberies, house burning, and such like enormities and crimes" and opposing the proslavery Lecompton Constitution, then pending in Congress, on the grounds that it had not been fairly voted on by the people of Kansas. Despite their opposition to the proslavery constitution, the men at the meeting wanted it clearly known that they rejected "with indignation and scorn the base attempts of a few government fed editors and unprincipled demagogues to class Union and conservative men with Abolitionists and Black Republicans for refusing to co-operate with the so-called National Democracy in their foul crusade against the Union."

Clearly, by 1858, allegiance to the Union was beginning to supplant allegiance to the Democratic Party as the predominant political sentiment in southwest Missouri. As the editor of the *Springfield Mirror* remarked in the wake of a second Union meeting a few weeks later, "The fact there is a party in the Southwest, so long the stronghold of the so-called National Democracy, in favor of the Union of the States, as they are, is becoming more and more manifest."

A third mass meeting of unionists in late May reaffirmed the resolutions of the first two meetings. The dedication to the Union, regardless of party, espoused by a growing number of men in Greene County and throughout the country in 1858, along with their mounting disgust with the secessionist faction of the Democratic Party, foretold both the rise of the Constitutional Union Party and the split in the Democratic Party that resulted in the nomination in 1860 of four different candidates for president of the United States.

In the state of Missouri as a whole, three distinct political camps developed during the months leading up to the Civil War. The Unconditional Unionists, a good number of whom were also abolitionists, vowed to support the Union regardless of what might happen. They made up a relatively small portion of the state's people and were concentrated in the St. Louis area, principal home to Missouri's fiercely loyal German population. The secessionists formed another small minority of the state's population. They dominated in certain rural areas throughout the state and were represented disproportionately in the state legislature. The overwhelming majority of Missouri's citizens, however, were Conservative or Conditional Unionists. Many of them had ties to the South, and most opposed abolition but pledged to support the Union as long as the Federal government did not invade or otherwise coerce the Southern states.

The 1860 presidential election results in Missouri illustrate this three-way political division in the state and the ascendancy of the middle-of-the-road position. Abraham Lincoln, the Republican candidate, received only 17,028 votes in the state, and John C. Breckinridge, the candidate of the Southern Democrats, received only 31,317. Meanwhile, the two centrist candidates, Stephen Douglas of the Northern Democrats and John Bell of the Constitutional Union Party, received more than 58,000 votes each.

Conservative Unionism dominated in southwest Missouri and Greene County, as it did in the state as a whole. The Constitutional Union ticket, which featured Judge Orr as the gubernatorial candidate, was particularly strong in Greene County, where Bell, endorsed by the *Springfield Mirror*, polled 986 votes. Breckinridge received 414 votes and had the endorsement of the *Springfield Equal Rights Gazette*, which had recently been started specifically to promote the Southern Democrats. Douglas garnered only 298 votes, despite the support of Springfield's leading newspaper, the *Springfield Advertiser*, while Lincoln received a mere 42. (The Republican party had gotten not a single vote in Greene County in the 1856 election.)

As suggested by Lincoln's meager vote total in Greene County, "Republicans in Southwestern Missouri in 1860 were," in the words of Holcombe's county history, "few in number and widely scattered." Republicanism was in such "bad odor" in Greene County that the party's

Abraham Lincoln received only forty-two votes in Greene County in 1860. *Courtesy of Library of Congress.*

few adherents resorted to meeting in secret for fear of being driven from their homes, and they developed a system of signs and grips by which they recognized one another. In fact, when it was announced that forty-two men in Greene County had voted for Lincoln, the number was considered remarkably large, as it had previously been thought that there were only a dozen or so Republicans in the county.

Not surprisingly, most Greene County citizens, therefore, greeted the news of Lincoln's victory in November 1860 with disapproval, but the large majority, including some of the men who had voted for Breckinridge, expressed strong support for the Union and resolved to abide by the result of the election. For some of them, though, this sentiment soon changed after South Carolina seceded in December and other Southern states followed. The very fact that most southwest Missourians were not extremists, but instead attempted to chart a middle-of-the-road course, sometimes caused them to vacillate. As the 1883 county history suggested, the only thing certain about the sentiments of men in those days was that "they were liable to change. Secessionists one week became Union men the next, and vice versa." Even in the face of the secession of the Southern states, however, the vast majority of Greene County residents and other southwest Missourians still hoped that civil war could be avoided, and they adopted a wait-and-see attitude.

They didn't have to wait long. In early January 1861, retiring Missouri governor Robert Stewart, in his farewell message, urged a middle-of-the-road course of "armed neutrality" for his state, a position that reflected the views of the majority of the people, but incoming governor Claiborne F. Jackson declared in his inaugural speech that Missouri's interests lay with the seceding states. He, however, recommended a state convention that would allow the people of Missouri and their representatives to decide for themselves the issue of secession.

The election of delegates to the convention took place in mid-February. In the Nineteenth Senatorial District (which included Greene County), Union candidates Sample Orr and Littleberry Hendricks of Springfield and R.W. Jamison of Webster County defeated the three secessionist candidates, including N.F. Jones and Jabez Owen (son-in-law of Springfield founder John Polk Campbell) of Greene County, by a margin of about four to one, each polling about 80 percent of the vote. (Holcombe's 1883 Greene County history called the unionists "unconditional Union" men and the secessionists "conditional Union" men. However, most of the so-called conditional Union men harbored secessionist sentiments, and even a good number of the unconditional Union men, as the author admitted, later ended up fighting on the Confederate side or at least sympathizing with the Southern cause.) Meeting in St. Louis in early March, the state convention voted overwhelmingly to stay in the Union but also adopted a resolution opposing any attempt by the Federal government to coerce the seceding states or the use of military force by either side. During the first few months of 1861, the growing national divide stirred the people of Springfield and Greene County to take a keen interest in political affairs. They freely discussed the possibility of civil war, and some people began preparing for such an eventuality. A few openly sympathized with the seceding states, but most continued to espouse the Conservative Union position, declaring that they were neither secessionists nor abolitionists.

The prospect of war during the early months of 1861 not only generated lively public discussion but also prompted Union men and secessionists alike to begin organizing and holding meetings throughout the county. Robert P. Matthews, who joined a "Union League" in Greene County during the months leading up to the war, recalled, "All these organizations were mainly of a secret nature, meeting at night with guarded doors, and a system of passwords, ceremonies known only to the initiated." Such precautions, he explained, were not necessary in the Deep South or the upper Northern states, where nearly everyone was of the same mind. "But here on the border it was quite different. You did not know who was friend or who was foe."

One of the larger prewar unionist meetings in the area was held near the end of March in the southwest part of Greene County near the Christian County line, not far from where the Battle of Wilson's Creek was later fought. Prominent citizens from throughout southwest Missouri, including Littleberry Hendricks and Marcus Boyd from Springfield, attended as delegates to discuss the state of affairs in their respective counties.

The secessionists, although in the minority, were equally active. On the evening of March 25, N.F. Jones gave a speech to a secessionist gathering on the Springfield square, and the group, according to the *Advertiser*, promenaded on the streets "under a strange flag." Three days later, on the twenty-eighth, U.S. Treasurer W.C. Price, a former Greene County probate judge, returned to Springfield from Washington and joined a demonstration of secessionists in another procession, this one headed by a small brass band. On Saturday afternoon, March 30, a larger group of secessionists gathered in Springfield, and a Confederate flag was raised over a private residence. Some of the Union men of the town became indignant, and the two sides had a standoff with pistols drawn before the flag was taken down, and the two parties dispersed without bloodshed or violence.

Even as mounting tension between unionists and secessionists led to incidents like the late March standoff in Springfield, and even as men on both sides prepared for war, most residents of Greene County continued to hope that such a calamity might be averted—or at least that Missouri might be able to stay out the conflict. The Confederate bombardment of Fort Sumter on April 12, 1861, however, destroyed any prospect of compromise or remaining neutral. Like the rest of the country, southwest Missouri would be drawn into a great civil war, whether its people liked it or not.

Chapter 2

The Guns of Fort Sumter Echo in Springfield

Springfield received word of the attack on Fort Sumter by telegraph, and the *Advertiser* ran an extra edition announcing the event. Stirred to intense excitement by the news, the townspeople huddled on every corner, discussing the incident and what it might mean for the future course of the country.

In response to the firing on Fort Sumter, President Lincoln issued a call for seventy-five thousand troops to repress the rebellion, and Missouri was asked to furnish four regiments as its share. Governor Jackson refused to comply, denouncing Lincoln's call to arms as an "unholy crusade." Instead, the governor got a resolution passed through the Missouri legislature condemning any Federal attempt to coerce the seceding states, and he also began trying to organize a state militia for the defense of Missouri against possible invasion. Although lawmakers balked at approving the latter effort, Southern sympathizers throughout the state nonetheless began organizing under the proposed "military bill," and a group seized the Federal arsenal at Liberty, Missouri, on April 20 to arm the budding militia.

Loyalists throughout the state also began organizing and arming themselves as home guard forces, and they were particularly active in Springfield and Greene County, where Unionism was more dominant than in many other parts of the state. Springfieldian John S. Phelps, congressman from Missouri's Sixth District (which included Greene

A future governor of Missouri, John S. Phelps was a prominent Union man in Springfield during the Civil War. *From Holcombe's* History of Greene County, Missouri.

County), hurried home from Washington at the outset of the war, and on Saturday, May 4, he and other prominent citizens (like Judge Orr) addressed a large Union meeting at the bank building on the north side of the Springfield square. Toward the end of the meeting, an Arkansas man named A.M. Bedford was given an opportunity to present the secessionist point of view.

The incumbent postmaster at Springfield, Nathan Robinson, was a secessionist, and near the beginning of the war he had begun flying a Rebel flag over the post office, located on the south side of the square. In early May, Benjamin Kite, a Republican who had voted for Lincoln, received a commission to replace Robinson as postmaster of Springfield. Arming himself with a pistol, Kite marched into the post office and demanded possession of it, presenting both his commission and his pistol as his authority. Robinson did not resist, quickly gave up his keys to the post office, and took down the secessionist flag.

When a party of about seven hundred of Governor Jackson's nascent state militia camped on the outskirts of St. Louis near another Federal armory in early May, Captain Nathaniel Lyon, who had been organizing and training troops in the St. Louis area for the Federal government,

Benjamin Kite took over as Springfield postmaster at the beginning of the Civil War. *Courtesy of History Museum for Springfield–Greene County.*

feared that the militia might be planning to seize the armory the same way it had done at Liberty. On May 10, Lyon disarmed the militiamen at Camp Jackson (so named in honor of the governor) and was marching them as prisoners through the streets of St. Louis when angry pro-Southern demonstrators gathered and started pelting the Federal soldiers with rocks and other debris. Some of the inexperienced Federal soldiers rashly opened fire, killing almost thirty protesters, including two women and a child. This incident infuriated Southern sympathizers throughout the state and drove even many Conditional Unionists into the Southern camp. The state legislature now quickly approved Governor Jackson's efforts to raise a state militia under the military bill. General Sterling Price, former governor of the state, was given command of the force, dubbed the Missouri State Guard, and General James S. Rains, a Sarcoxie politician, was placed in command of the Eighth District, which encompassed most of southwest Missouri. In Springfield, the *Equal Rights Gazette* scoffed at the notion of "armed neutrality" and urged Missouri to side with the South.

Despite the Camp Jackson affair, however, the unionists of Greene County largely remained loyal. On May 18, they assembled on the public square in Springfield, about one thousand strong, many of them armed with rifles. John S. Phelps again addressed the gathering, as did other prominent Union men, including Marcus Boyd and his son, S.H. "Pony" Boyd. Some of the speakers discussed Governor Jackson's military bill, which called for able-bodied men to enroll in the Missouri State Guard and outlawed any militia units except those authorized by state guard commanders. Many in the Springfield crowd declared that they would not submit to the new law. Toward the end of the meeting, the Union

Later a Federal colonel, Springfield lawyer S.H. "Pony" Boyd wrote letters and gave speeches in support of the Union at the beginning of the Civil War. *Courtesy of History Museum for Springfield–Greene County.*

speakers, as they had done two weeks earlier, extended an invitation for those with opposing views to address the gathering. Accepting the offer, Jabez Owen rose in opposition to the previous speakers, but he was then rebutted by another Union orator.

A few days later, a company of 250 armed men from Christian County and the south part of Greene County galloped into Springfield in support of the Union men of the town because a rumor had circulated in Christian County that the military bill was to be enforced at Springfield and that one or two loyal men were going to be hanged. "We are happy to say that there was no truth to the reports," noted the *Advertiser* at the time, "and hence the assistance of our friends was not needed. We mention this little incident only to show the feeling that pervades the people of Christian, and their readiness to resist oppression. We doubt not the citizens of Greene county are with them in this sentiment."

In an effort to keep the war out of Missouri, General Price met in St. Louis with General William S. Harney, commanding the Union army's Department of the West, and reached an agreement on May 21 that Federal troops would not interfere in state affairs. In return, Price would preserve the peace in Missouri, and the enlistment of men in the state guard would be suspended.

After news of the accord reached southwest Missouri, the loyal men of the region rested easier for a few days until some of them reported being harassed by secessionists. Also, Union intelligence indicated that the state guard was continuing to organize and prepare for war despite the Price-Harney agreement. John S. Phelps and other prominent Springfield citizens complained of these abuses to General Harney, who relayed the concerns to General Price on May 24. Harney said that he would be forced to send troops to southwest Missouri or authorize Union home guards in the region if the acts of aggression against Union men and the organization of the state guard did not cease. (In fact, Union home guard forces were already organizing throughout the state, even without official authorization.) Price replied by telegraph the same day, assuring Harney that the reports he had received were no doubt incorrect and that, if not, Price would take care of the situation and carry out the terms of their agreement faithfully.

Almost a week later, however, the situation in southwest Missouri was still tense. From his Springfield home on May 30, former Missouri secretary of state John M. Richardson wrote to O.D. Filley, a prominent Union man in St. Louis, "Everything is quiet here, but both parties appear feverish and restless. The Union men hope the Price and Harney arrangement may be carried out, but they have no confidence in its being done."

Pony Boyd also wrote to Filley on May 30, complaining that Rains was still enlisting men in southwest Missouri for the state guard, that some of his men had threatened to attack a Union home guard force in neighboring Dade County if it did not disband, that secessionists in southwest Missouri had been ordering loyal citizens to leave and that the Union people were "overwhelmed with terror and fright."

Receiving little satisfaction in response to their complaints, the Union men of Springfield began patrolling the streets and guarding the roads leading into town to prevent the Rebels from coming in and taking away gunpowder and other supplies. If part of the purpose of the Union activity was to discourage the opposition, it seemingly had the desired effect. Southern sympathizer P.S. Wilkes, writing from Springfield on June 3, 1861, to an acquaintance in St. Louis, noted, "We are overwhelmed and our men are overawed and dispirited, while the other side are haughty and defiant…We must do something to inspire confidence in our side and make the other feel that Springfield is not every place." Wilkes went on to suggest that Springfield and Greene County needed help from the more Southern-sympathizing counties of Missouri.

The Southern forces in the Springfield area were not quite as dispirited as the letter writer believed. In early June, under orders from General Rains, enrollees in the Missouri State Guard from throughout southwest Missouri began gathering at the Fulbright Spring (near the present-day intersection of College and Fort Streets) on the west edge of Springfield to organize and train. According to Union reports, between six and seven hundred "secessionists," some from as far away as one hundred miles, trekked into town for the occasion, which culminated with a barbecue and mass meeting at the spring on June 11.

On the same day, the unionists, who had learned of the Rebel meeting ahead of time and did not want to be outdone, gathered (1,200–1,500 strong) at Goose Pond on the Kickapoo Prairie (near the present-day intersection of National and Sunset). "Hither they came from all points of the compass by hundreds," according to Holcombe, "bringing with them

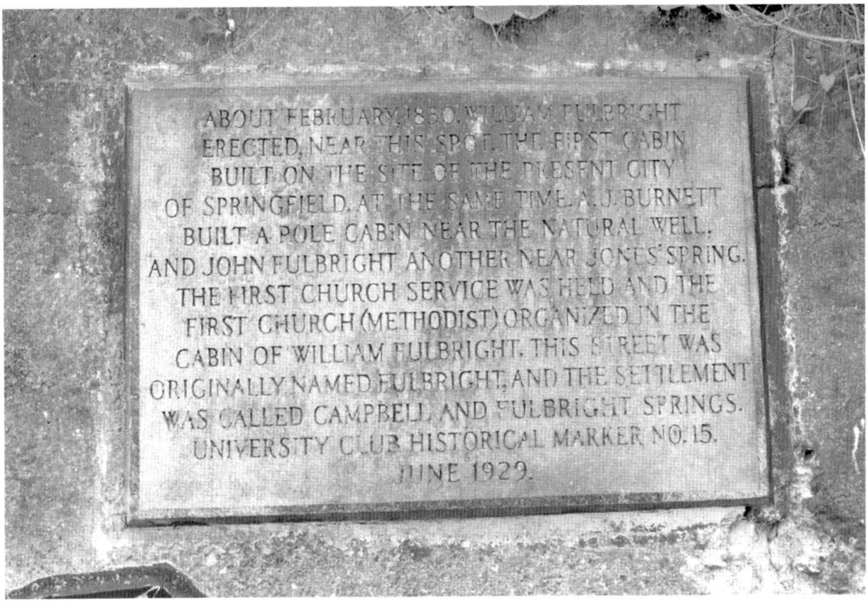

Historic marker on West College Street near the location of Fulbright Spring, which served as a gathering place during the Civil War. *Photo by author.*

their arms, their horses, their wagons, and their provisions." Because of the heat of the day and the lack of shade and water in the area, they soon removed to John S. Phelps's farm, encompassing the area of today's Phelps Grove Park, closer to town. Here the unionists organized into the Greene and Christian County Home Guard, with Phelps as colonel of the regiment, Marcus Boyd as lieutenant-colonel, and Sample Orr and Pony Boyd as majors. (Before this time, the home guard units in the region had been independent of one another and had no organization or leadership beyond the company level.) Some members of the newly formed unit wanted to ride across town immediately and attack the state guard forces that were organizing at Fulbright Spring, but Phelps vetoed such an action, suggesting that fighting and bloodshed would come soon enough without deliberately precipitating a battle now.

The Southerners, who wished to make a show of force, prepared in the afternoon to parade through downtown Springfield onto the square. There they wanted to raise above the courthouse a Rebel flag, which had been made especially for the occasion. However, messengers had been passing between the two camps all day, and the Rebels knew that

Marker at Phelps Grove Park commemorating the important role of the Phelps farm during the Civil War in Springfield. *Photo by author.*

hoisting a Southern flag would likely result in a fight right in the heart of Springfield, endangering their friends and loved ones.

Missouri State Guard captain Leonidas St. Clair "Dick" Campbell, nephew of Springfield founder John Polk Campbell and one of the leading spirits of the mass meeting at Fulbright Spring, volunteered to go as a delegate to the Phelps farm and meet with the home guard officers regarding the state guard's desire to raise a Southern flag. At the Union camp, Phelps told him that no such flag should be raised in Greene County. Campbell then proposed hoisting a Missouri state flag, and Phelps agreed but insisted that a U.S. flag would have to be raised above the state flag. This compromise averted bloodshed, both flags were shortly afterward raised above the courthouse, and both sides paraded on the square.

Other accounts of this incident suggest that negotiations between the two sides were a bit more hostile than this cited version of events might indicate. A teenage lad living in Springfield during the Civil War, William Rountree, recalled years later, for instance, that both the home guard and the Rebels marched onto the square at about the same time: "It looked as if war was going to begin right then. John Payne, a rabid Rebel, was making a speech from the top of the courthouse, and Pony Boyd, a loyal young lawyer, was making a Union speech from the steps of the courthouse. One demanded he be permitted to raise the flag and the other that he be prevented." Only when a clash seemed imminent did peacemakers intercede and permit the raising of a flag by the Southern side.

Francis P. Blair Jr., U.S. congressman from St. Louis, and Captain Lyon had been suspicious of the Price-Harney agreement from the beginning and considered it little more than a ruse on the part of Price and Jackson to give them time to train and equip the state guard troops. Blair influenced President Lincoln to replace Harney with Lyon, who had been promoted to brigadier general, and Harney was relieved of duty on May 31. On June 11, the same day as the flag incident in Springfield, Price and Jackson met with the new Union general in St. Louis in the hopes of continuing the terms of the Price-Harney agreement, but the fiery Lyon was in no mood for compromise and essentially declared war on the still-loyal state of Missouri.

As soon as Price and Jackson had been escorted beyond the Union lines at St. Louis, Lyon dispatched three Federal regiments to southwest Missouri to secure the region for the Union and cut off a possible southerly retreat by the state guard. At the same time, troops under Lyon's immediate command pursued Price and Jackson up the Missouri River toward Boonville, where the first skirmish of the Civil War in Missouri was fought on June 17.

Meanwhile, just a few days after the flag incident in Springfield, three local Union men slipped out of town, under cover of darkness to avoid being intercepted by Rebel forces, on a clandestine mission to St. Louis. Lewis Crenshaw, Edwin Robberson, and Pony Boyd wanted to impress on Federal authorities there the necessity of immediately sending troops to southwest Missouri to protect loyal families and to help the Union men of the region hold it against the gathering state guard forces. At Rolla, they met the first of the troops Lyon had dispatched to southwest Missouri, already on their way to Springfield under Colonel Franz Sigel. After resting in Rolla for one night, Colonel Sigel, accompanied by the three Greene County envoys, took up the march for Springfield on June 21.

Chapter 3

The Yankee Dutch Come to Town

Sigel reached Springfield on June 24. Although the troops were sopping wet from a recent cloudburst, dressed in tatters, and tired from the journey, the ragged outfit marched proudly into town with a brass band leading the way, and many Union citizens of Springfield turned out to hail their arrival. A German soldier in Sigel's command, John T. Buegel, recorded in his diary that the residents of Springfield were mainly Union sympathizers and that they "greeted us in a most friendly manner."

While it is true that Springfield was predominantly a Union town, it was now made more so by the fact that many Southern sympathizers had left upon learning of the Federals' approach. Two days before Sigel's arrival, the *Springfield Journal* had reported "a continuous succession of flight from this place of the most active and violent Secessionists."

Also, some citizens of Missouri, and presumably of Springfield, professed loyalty while secretly harboring secessionist sentiments. As an Iowa newspaper correspondent observed from Springfield one month after Sigel's arrival, many of the people of Missouri were "governed by fear and interest, and are Union or secession as the strong side goes."

To the few openly secessionist residents remaining in Springfield, like those at the Christian Church, the sight of Sigel's men marching into town was not a welcome spectacle. According to Escott's *History and Directory of Springfield and North Springfield*, it was a Sunday morning when Sigel's men came into town, and a detachment of soldiers under an unidentified German major marched straightway to the church, where secessionist pastor Charles Carlton and his predominantly secessionist congregation were gathered for services. The soldiers surrounded the building, and as soon as services ended, the major stepped into the doorway and announced in a booming voice and with a strong German accent that he was placing the men of the congregation under arrest in the name of the United States and the president, by the power of the army, and by the orders of Colonel Franz Sigel. The congregation, according to Escott, "were never more attentive listeners to any sermon than to that one, nor more obedient to any advice than they were to the Dutch major on that occasion," and they promptly passed out of the church single file and were marched as prisoners to the courthouse on the public square.

Franz Sigel and his "Yankee Dutch" soldiers arrived in Springfield on June 24, 1861. Colonel Franz Sigel, #31852, in the collection of Wilson's Creek National Battlefield. *Courtesy of National Park Service.*

The only problem with Escott's colorful account is that if Sigel had arrived on a Sunday, it would mean that he arrived on June 23, but the most credible evidence suggests that he arrived on Monday, June 24, or perhaps even a day later. Therefore, it is probable that the meeting at the church occurred on a weekday. Louisa Cheairs McKinney, granddaughter of John Polk Campbell, was present at the meeting and recalled years later that it was one of a series of "basket revivals" being held throughout the week. Louisa also remembered that the Southern sympathizers at the church were pointed out to the Federal soldiers by two men in the congregation who had previously been friends and neighbors of her family but "were now our enemies." Although Louisa, the other children, and the women of the congregation were not arrested, they trailed alongside their loved ones as the men were marched to the public square. When twelve-year-old Louisa and her grandmother, Louisa Campbell (widow of John Polk Campbell), got back home, they found that one of the elder Louisa's sons, Sam Campbell, had run off to join the Southern army and another, Tom Campbell, was making preparations to join.

Arrests similar to those at the Christian Church were made throughout Springfield, and soon the courthouse was nearly full. Sigel appointed John S. Phelps and Marcus Boyd as commissioners to evaluate the cases of the men arrested as traitors. As prominent and unquestionably loyal citizens, they were given authority to release any prisoners they saw fit and to keep in jail only those who had committed blatant acts of disloyalty or who refused to take an oath of allegiance to the Union. Consequently, many of those arrested were soon released, and only the most guilty and unrepentant Rebels were kept in the lockup.

In addition to capturing numerous men suspected of disloyalty, the Federal troops, upon their arrival in Springfield, also seized a good deal of property from the town's citizens. A stash of gunpowder was taken from Dick Campbell's barn, for instance. Although it was mainly the property of known Rebels like Campbell that was targeted for confiscation, other citizens were sometimes subjected to having their animals or other property impressed.

These abuses aggravated the natural antipathy that the German soldiers under Sigel and the citizens of Springfield, especially those with Southern ties, felt toward each other. Neither side understood nor trusted the other. The townspeople had cheered the sight of Sigel marching into town only because his men were Union soldiers who might provide welcome protection from rabid secessionists. However, to Ozarkians, even Conservative Unionists, the St. Louis Germans were foreigners who scarcely spoke the same language, and most out-state Missourians considered all of them fanatic abolitionists, whether they were or not. In short, they were "damned Yankee Dutch," as locals often called them. Many of the Germans, on the other hand, could hardly conceive how an avid supporter of slavery could also be a supporter of the Union, but most Greene County citizens were both.

A few days after his arrival, Sigel departed for Sarcoxie, with some of his men riding horses and wagons "pressed" from the citizens of Springfield for the service of the government. Left at Springfield were two companies of Colonel Frederick Salomon's regiment under Major Ferdinand Cronenbold, acting commander of the post. At the Battle of Carthage on July 5, Sigel was defeated by Jackson's state guard, and he beat a hasty retreat back to Springfield.

In the meantime, Captain Thomas W. Sweeny had arrived in Springfield from St. Louis on July 1 with additional Federal troops and, as an "elected" brigadier general of volunteers, had taken charge of the forces in southwest Missouri. On July 4, he issued a proclamation assuring the citizens of southwest Missouri that his troops were in their midst not

Captain Thomas W. Sweeny was an acting brigadier general when he came to Springfield the first of July 1861. Captain Thomas W. Sweeny, #32009, in the collection of Wilson's Creek National Battlefield. *Courtesy of National Park Service.*

as enemies but as friends for their protection. Promising those who might be suspected of disloyalty that they would be treated fairly, he urged them to appear before him or one of his officers to take an oath of allegiance.

Holcombe's 1883 Greene County history noted wryly that the Federal commanders were fond of issuing proclamations during the early part of the war but that the edicts had little effect because the secessionists disregarded them and the Loyalists did not need them. While admitting that the Southern leaders also "favored this method of fighting enemies," the author declared that "Sweeny's Springfield proclamation was about as effectual as the noted bull of the Pope against the comet."

Sweeny apparently found few Southern sympathizers in Greene County—or few, at any rate, who were willing to take him up on his recommendation that they swear an oath. On July 12, he reported to St. Louis that he had found the residents of Springfield and surrounding area "generally loyal." He complained, however, that his troops were "very deficient in ammunition."

General Lyon's march south after the skirmish at Boonville was delayed by rain-swollen rivers, but in early July, he linked up in Henry County with a force of army regulars and Kansas volunteers under Major Samuel D. Sturgis and, on July 13, finally reached Springfield, where he took charge of the combined Federal force of more than seven thousand men who were now in the vicinity. When Lyon first got to the area, he rode into Springfield on horseback with an escort of ten men. Soon afterward, he established his headquarters at a house owned by Congressman Phelps located on College Street west of the square, and he set up living quarters at a house on Jefferson several blocks away.

While Lyon was establishing his headquarters in Springfield, his men went into camp near Pond Spring in the western part of the county, a couple of miles north of present-day Republic. These men, along with the Federals who had arrived earlier, formed a roughly semicircular arc that stretched from the area of Pond Spring and Little York to just south of Springfield. (The small village of Little York was located about one mile east of Pond Spring or about the same distance west of present-day Brookline.) Generally speaking, Sweeny's men were camped close to Springfield, while the new arrivals under Lyon and Sturgis were farther west.

Although Lyon's men were not as deficient in arms and ammunition as Sweeny said his were, all of the Federal troops were poorly clothed. An Iowa soldier in Lyon's command, writing to his hometown newspaper in Muscatine, said of the soldiers in his company that some had "bare feet, blistered and scalded; some with shoes without heels or toes—others without sides or soles; boots cut down and cut for the accommodation of blisters and corns; trousers with original seats gone—a few replaced with carpeting, coffee sacks or flannel; others with fronts of legs gone…others worn out around the feet, inside of the legs, and torn to the knees."

The Union troops were as ill-fed as they were clothed, and they subsisted on one-quarter rations much of the time they were in the Springfield area. William Branson, another Iowa soldier, wrote in his diary shortly after he and his comrades arrived in Greene County that "[o]ne cracker, coffee without sugar, and beef constitutes a meal."

Even beef was a scarcity, and the coffee was quickly gone as well. The Iowans soon dubbed their camp at Pond Spring "Camp Mush," recalled Eugene F. Ware, a comrade of Branson's, because they rarely got anything to eat other than cornmeal and water. When one of the Iowa boys happened upon a blackberry patch on a nearby farm, he foraged a hatful of blackberries and brought them into camp, where they were quickly consumed as a delicacy. Later in the summer, when Ware and his fellow soldiers were almost out of rations, they boiled blackberry roots for the little sustenance they could provide.

Clean water, too, was a luxury that few of the soldiers enjoyed. Ralph Zublin, yet another Iowa soldier, writing to his wife back in Dubuque, declared, "We are very short of water and soap, and the effect may be imagined. A more dirty lot of savages was never seen." Describing his recent encounter with a snake that had crawled onto his blanket, he declared that the many snakes in the region were also a nuisance, but he concluded by reemphasizing, "Water is the great trouble. We have great difficulty in getting it. A small stream is 'nowhere' for a body of men nearly 6,000 strong, and choking for want of water."

When Lyon found upon reaching Springfield that the supplies he had ordered had not arrived ahead of him, he promptly sent a message to Colonel Chester Harding Jr. at the St. Louis arsenal emphasizing that "[s]hoes, shirts, blouses, etc. are much wanted, and I would have you furnish them, if possible, in considerable quantities."

Two days later, on July 15, Major John M. Schofield, Lyon's acting adjutant general, also implored Harding to send relief to Springfield. "All idea of any further advance movement," the major said, "or of even maintaining our present position, must soon be abandoned unless the Government furnish us promptly with large re-enforcements and supplies. Our troops are badly clothed, poorly fed, and imperfectly supplied with tents. None of them have as yet been paid, and the three-months volunteers have become disheartened to such extent that very few of them are willing to renew their enlistment."

The pleas by Lyon and his fellow officers for reinforcements and supplies fell on deaf ears, partly because the Union military structure in Missouri was in a state of flux. In early July, a new Western Department was created, and Major General John C. Fremont, a hero of the Mexican-American War and the 1856 Republican presidential nominee, was named its commander. However, Fremont did not reach his St. Louis headquarters until July 25. In the meantime, during mid-July, Lyon sent several requests for additional support directly to Washington, but these petitions, too, like his appeal to Harding, yielded no results.

Like Private Buegel and his German comrades who had reached Springfield in late June, the soldiers who arrived in Greene County with Lyon in mid-July were favorably impressed with the unionist sentiments and the friendliness of most Greene County residents, but their admiration for the locals, like that of the Germans, often did not extend beyond the realm of politics and casual amicability. For example, L.L. Jones, a Kansas soldier in Sturgis's command, writing back home the day after Lyon's arrival in the Springfield area, remarked approvingly on the unionist feelings of the people and the "fertile and beautiful" countryside with "many fine farms," but, he added, "The people are very ignorant."

Despite the undercurrent of tension that sometimes colored the dealings between local citizens and occupying soldiers, most residents got along reasonably well with the men of Lyon's army. Not long after Lyon's men had gone into camp, for example, a party of men and women from Springfield went out to the campsite west of town to treat the officers to a picnic, and just as the members of the group had spread their basket dinners on the ground and were partaking of the meal, the festivities were interrupted when a great cloud of dust was spotted on the western horizon. Since Price and Confederate general Ben McCulloch were known to be not far away in that direction, the approaching column was assumed to be the advance guard of the Southern army. The sight disrupted the picnic and caused the troops to prepare for battle, but the alarm proved to be a false one. The caravan that had stirred up the dust turned out to be Union men, women, and children who had been frightened out of Barry, McDonald, and Newton Counties by the state guard troops and were seeking refuge in Springfield.

The destitute condition of the Federal troops at Springfield, of course, led to increased plundering, and much of General Lyon's time was taken up by area citizens besieging him with claims for property that had been taken by his troops. By late July, pillaging had become such a problem that Lyon was forced to issue an order declaring that the property of law-abiding citizens should not be molested and stating his determination to suppress incidents of "plundering, wanton destruction of property, and disregard of personal rights" such as those of which he had recently been informed. The general made it clear that his order applied to all citizens, regardless of their sympathies, as long as they were not in arms against the Union or exciting others to open rebellion. Even citizens who were openly disloyal would have their property seized only on proper authority and for the purpose of disarming them and disrupting their ability to make mischief against the government, not for the mere sake of harming families or wantonly destroying property.

Despite his proclamation to the contrary, Lyon sometimes looked the other way when his men stole property from the homes or farms of local citizens to supply their own needs, especially if the locals were known to be or suspected of being disloyal. R.I. Holcombe, the editor of the 1883 Greene County history, for instance, while allowing that Lyon generally treated the people of Springfield "with courtesy and kindness," lamented the fact that he also allowed the property of citizens to be impressed "to some extent."

On the other hand, citizens of the Springfield area sometimes took advantage of the troops' dire situation by charging inflated prices, both for food sold to individual soldiers and for grain sold to Federal purchasing agents for processing at local mills to feed the troops. On

July 18, William Branson, the Iowa soldier who had earlier grumbled about the scant government rations, complained that the army had run out of bread and that the soldiers were being forced to buy their own provisions "at an exorbitant price." A few days later, he explained that area farmers were "now making it a practice of bringing in loads of provisions—pies, biscuits, cornbread—and selling them to us soldiers for two prices knowing that we are short of eatables."

Also, even though Lyon might have overlooked, for example, the theft of apples from a local orchard, he did not allow the plundering of Springfield businesses, and city storekeepers sometimes took advantage of the Federals' want of food and supplies by selling their merchandise at higher-than-normal prices.

Not all the local people, though, tried to take advantage of the Federals' dire situation. For example, the very next day after complaining about the farmers who were charging exorbitant prices for their goods, Private Branson rejoiced that pies and cornbread were "in abundance in camp today and selling at reasonable prices." Also, Mary Phelps, wife of Colonel Phelps, reportedly handed out food each day from the Phelps farm free of charge to the soldiers camped at Springfield.

For the soldiers camped on the outskirts of town, getting to come into Springfield was a rare occasion. On July 20, for instance, the Iowa regiment was marched into town, and a lot of mail from home awaited the men. Private Ware received two letters from his father, each containing a five-dollar bill. Ware celebrated by treating himself and two of his pals to all they could eat at a local restaurant. He then went into a confectionery store and drank all the soda water he could hold. Later, he bought a woolen shirt, a cotton bandana, a new pair of shoestrings, and some candy. He washed up at a local hotel and then loaned his friends the rest of his money.

The festive mood was soon shattered, however. Because their ninety-day term of enlistment had expired, the Iowans were under the impression they had been marched to Springfield to be mustered out of service. Instead, a bugle call summoned them into formation about midafternoon, and the disillusioned soldiers were soon marching south on a dubious expedition to Forsyth under General Sweeny to clean out the Rebels supposed to be infesting the town.

The severe situation caused by lack of food and supplies at Springfield was exacerbated by other problems during mid- to late July. An outbreak of typhoid fever among the troops, caused at least in part by drinking creek water, forced Lyon to turn the unfinished courthouse at the northwest corner of the square into a hospital, and it was soon overflowing with sick soldiers. Exasperated that they had not been paid, about two thousand Union volunteers, many of them Germans from St. Louis, refused to reenlist at the expiration of their ninety-day term, and they marched out of Springfield and headed home. A steady stream of civilian refugees, such as those from the southwest corner of Missouri whose approach had disturbed the picnic, continued to spill into town with hungry bellies.

In late July, Lyon finally organized a wagon train of refugees and ailing soldiers and sent it to Rolla under the escort of Colonel Phelps and a detachment of his home guard. Phelps also bore a message from Lyon to General Fremont at St. Louis in which Lyon renewed his request for additional men and supplies, trying once again to impress on Fremont the urgency of the situation in southwest Missouri. Despite the personal entreaties of Phelps and other envoys dispatched by Lyon, Fremont, believing that he needed all his resources to thwart the possibility of Confederates coming up the Mississippi River to threaten St. Louis, still offered no relief.

Near the end of July, Lyon's scouts reported that a large Rebel force under General Price and Confederate general Ben McCulloch was concentrating at Cassville, from where it would likely move up toward Springfield along the Wire Road (so called because of the telegraph line that stretched along it). Considering that Lyon was greatly outnumbered, that his weary troops were in poor condition for a fight, and that reinforcements were not likely to be forthcoming, the logical thing to do might have been to retreat. The zealous Lyon, though, was not the retreating type, and the volunteers were itching for a fight or else to be allowed to go home. Lyon resolved to go out and meet the enemy.

Chapter 4

Wilson's Creek

A Perfect Panic

On the afternoon of August 1, Lyon's entire force of about 5,800 soldiers marched out of Springfield on the Wire Road, except for a small detachment of home guard and volunteers left behind to guard the town. The Federals camped that evening on Wilson Creek, about ten miles southwest of Springfield, and then continued the march the next day. On the morning of August 2, the Union advance skirmished briefly with a scouting party of Rebels, and late that afternoon, the Federals had a sharper skirmish with the Rebel vanguard under General Rains at Dug Springs, about three miles southwest of present-day Clever. The next day, Lyon continued down the Wire Road before deciding to turn back, and the return march to Springfield began on the morning of August 4.

Although the weather had been hot during July, the temperatures soared even higher, to near 110 degrees during the early days of August, and some of the soldiers died of heatstroke or dropped by the wayside, delirious with heat exhaustion. An Iowa soldier, writing home on August 5, said, "The weather here is intensely hot…These last five days have been almost intolerable to us Northerners. Indeed yesterday not less than 200 of our boys of the Iowa regiment fell out of ranks completely debilitated and unable to move." Journalist Thomas Knox, who accompanied the march to and from Dug Springs, wrote at the end of the war that he "passed scores of men who had fallen from utter exhaustion. Many were delirious, and begged piteously for water in ever so small a quantity. Several died from excessive heat, and others were for a long time unfit for duty."

When the march reached the Springfield area on the afternoon of August 5, Lyon left a rear guard of more than two thousand men under Major Sturgis four miles west of town at an outpost dubbed Camp Hunter, while the rest of the dusty and weary troops straggled into Springfield and slept on their arms that night.

After Lyon got back to Springfield, he met on the evening of August 5 with his top officers and a few of the leading citizens of Springfield at his headquarters on College Street to discuss what should be done next. Captain John S. Cavender, whom Lyon had earlier dispatched to St. Louis, had just returned to Springfield, and the captain reported that he had been granted a brief interview with General Fremont but that the general had already closed his office when Cavender arrived as scheduled for a promised second interview. The general's adjutant had later assured Cavender that reinforcements and a paymaster were on their way to Springfield, but Lyon was not encouraged by the abrupt treatment his envoy had been accorded in St. Louis.

Lyon was eager to take the fight to the enemy, but he knew that his odds of winning were slim without reinforcements. He grew more and more agitated as it became increasingly clear that he would likely have to make do with the troops already available to him. At one point, according to Holcombe's county history, either during the August 5 meeting or at one near the same time, Lyon reportedly lost his temper and cursed Fremont violently. "Goddamn, General Fremont!" he exploded. "He is a worse enemy to me and the Union cause than Price and McCulloch and the whole damned tribe of rebels in this part of the state!"

After collapsing from exhaustion on the evening of August 5 upon their return from the Dug Springs expedition, Private Ware and his Iowa comrades were roused in the middle of the night and moved to a different location, and when they awoke on the morning of the sixth, Ware discovered that they were camped on the Phelps farm, where they were fed bread from a government wagon. During the next day or two, the Iowa troops moved from place to place about Springfield but camped more than once on the Phelps farm. On one occasion, Mary Phelps and her female servant brought a basket of tomatoes out to the troops. "Mrs.

Phelps was a very sympathetic woman," recalled Ware, "and we all liked her very much."

Word reached Springfield on August 6 that the Confederates under McCulloch had moved up the Wire Road and were now camped on Wilson Creek only ten miles southwest of town, and Lyon contemplated a surprise attack on the Rebels that very night. He marched out to Camp Hunter with a portion of his troops, but instead of launching the proposed assault, he decided to withdraw the whole Federal force to Springfield, including those who had been posted west of town under Sturgis. Despite their withdrawal, Springfield was still well guarded. All the roads leading to and from town were closely patrolled, and the main streets were barricaded. The guards let anyone who wished to enter town do so but allowed no one to leave without a pass, thereby ensuring that the Federals could receive intelligence about the gathering Southern forces but that potential Rebel spies would be prevented from carrying information to McCulloch and Price.

On August 6, the day after returning from the Dug Springs expedition, Private Ware observed what he called "a perfect panic going on…among the civilians," as refugees by the hundreds flocked into Springfield from every direction seeking protection in numbers during their flight north. (Ware may have gotten the date wrong, since other sources cite August 7 as the day of greatest alarm among civilians, or it is just as likely that the terror lasted more than one day.) Many of the men carried shotguns or rifles, and the evacuees were soon assembled into a quasi-military organization of their own and started toward Rolla in another big caravan, accompanied by a number of sick soldiers and a party of Springfield citizens who had decided not to await the outcome of the clash of armies that now seemed inevitable.

Whether they fled to Rolla or stayed behind, Springfieldians were now experiencing the hardships of war firsthand. As the 1883 county history observed, local residents had finally "come to realize what civil war meant. The peaceful citizens of one year ago were now soldiers, with arms in their hands seeking to blow out one another's brains or cut one another's throats. Peaceful fields were converted into military camps; dwelling houses were made hospitals; peaceful plow horses were harnessed to cannon carriages…while a great battle, sure to be fierce and bloody, was imminent and to be fought on Greene County soil."

On the evening of August 7, General Lyon and his officers met to discuss whether to abandon southwest Missouri and withdraw to Rolla or perhaps Fort Scott, Kansas. Lyon opposed the idea. The very thought of retreat rankled him, and he did not wish to forsake the loyal citizens of southwest Missouri. Most of his subordinate officers, however, argued for a withdrawal, and Lyon might have been convinced if not for General Sweeny's adamant insistence that the Federals should not retire without a fight. Sweeny not only rejected the notion of withdrawal but also favored attacking the Rebels as soon as possible. His fervent speech convinced most of the other officers that the Federals should make a stand, and it gave Lyon renewed confidence. The next morning, when Lyon was asked when the Federals were going to leave Springfield, he promptly replied, "Not until we are whipped out."

During the morning of August 8, Lyon's pickets west of Springfield sent word that the Southern army, twenty thousand strong, was advancing on Springfield and was within two miles of the Federal outpost. (The actual strength of the combined Southern force of Confederates under McCulloch, Missouri State Guard under Price, and Arkansas troops under General N. Bart Pearce was about twelve thousand.) Lyon's entire army was placed on alert, and contingency plans for a retreat, in case one became necessary, were made. Supply wagons were loaded and moved to the center of town, and the funds of the local branch of the State Bank of Missouri were removed from the bank and deposited in one of the wagons. Civilians as well as soldiers were astir with excitement. "The people here are all getting ready to go through to Rolla with us," wrote Private Branson in his August 8 diary entry.

The alarm, however, proved to be another false one. Instead of moving toward Springfield, the entire Rebel army was consolidating at Wilson Creek, and the next twenty-four hours passed with little ado, except for some minor skirmishing between opposing scouting parties about five miles west of Springfield.

On the morning of August 9, a courier arrived from St. Louis carrying a message, dated August 6, from General Fremont to General Lyon that no reinforcements were coming and that he would have to make do with the forces already at his disposal. Although no doubt fuming inside, Lyon calmly sent off a reply reiterating his desperate situation and expressing his fear that he would not be able to hold Springfield. Still determined, however, to launch a preemptive attack before the Rebels had a chance to move up and lay siege to Springfield, Lyon met with his officers later that day and announced that the Federal army would march at 6:00 p.m.

Again, Springfield was thrown into excitement. More wagons were loaded with goods in case retreat became necessary, and merchants and other citizens started giving away food to Union soldiers and wishing them good luck as they formed in town to begin their march to Wilson Creek.

Lyon, with most of the army, marched out of Springfield on the Mount Vernon Road (which generally followed the route of present-day Mount Vernon Street), while Colonel Sigel, who had convinced Lyon to divide his troops for a two-prong attack on the Rebels, left Camp Fremont south of town and marched down the Cassville or Wire Road with his brigade. Since plans called for each column to leave the main road a few miles west of town and march across the countryside, several local citizens accompanied the Federals as guides, including Lewis Crenshaw, one of the three men who had undertaken the mission to Rolla less than two months earlier seeking Union reinforcements for Springfield. Meanwhile, about 1,200 men of the Greene and Christian County Home Guard remained in Springfield to protect the town.

At dawn the next day, August 10, Lyon's army met the Confederate-allied forces in the first major battle of the Civil War west of the Mississippi. Both sides suffered relatively equal casualties during the fight, which raged for five hours. The Southerners lost an estimated 277 dead and almost 1,000 wounded (with no soldiers reported as missing), while the Federals lost about 285 dead and slightly over 1,000 in wounded and missing. General Lyon, however, was killed in the action, and because his army was eventually forced to retire, the battle was a Confederate victory. Widely termed the "Battle of Springfield" in initial newspaper reports and other communications, it came to be known as the Battle of Wilson's Creek or the Battle of Oak Hills, as the Southerners usually called it.

By August 10, many citizens of Springfield had already left for Rolla or another place of refuge, but those who remained, according to Franc Wilkie, a newspaperman accompanying the Union army, were "up long before daylight and awaiting with feverish anxiety the event of the day." Then, shortly after daylight, "the heavy boom of the artillery rolled through the town like the muttering of a thunder storm upon the horizon, and sent a thrill through every heart like a shock of electricity."

Anxiety continued to reign throughout the early morning as residents awaited word of how the battle was going. When the first wave of wounded men, who began pouring into town during the late morning while the battle yet raged, claimed that the Federals were driving the enemy back, the townspeople cheered and pitched in to help treat the wounded. Later arrivals, though, bore the news of General Lyon's death, and as the wounded kept streaming into town all day long—on foot, on horseback, and in ambulances and carriages of all description—it became increasingly clear that the battle had not gone well for the Union and that the evacuation of Springfield was likely.

Nathaniel Lyon led the Union forces at the Battle of Wilson's Creek and was killed in the action. General Nathaniel Lyon, #31765, in the collection of Wilson's Creek National Battlefield. *Courtesy the National Park Service.*

General Lyon had previously set up a hospital at the new courthouse in the charge of Dr. E.C. Franklin, surgeon of the Fifth Missouri Volunteers, but it and the adjacent sheriff's residence were quickly filled to capacity with about one hundred wounded men. The Bailey House Hotel, just off the square on South Street, was promptly converted to a hospital as well, but it, too, was soon full. Schools and churches, including the Methodist church at the corner of South and Walnut Streets, were then pressed into service. As many as thirty or forty private residences were also used as hospitals, but even these buildings were not sufficient to handle all the wounded, some of whom were merely laid out on the street. Wilkie

Dr. Samuel M. Melcher, who served as a surgeon in Springfield throughout much of the Civil War, brought Lyon's body back to town after the general was killed at Wilson's Creek. *From Holcombe's* History of Greene County, Missouri.

described the wounded as they were being brought into Springfield: "Some of the wounds were horrible; some had the lower jaw shot away, others had arms torn off, others came in with legs dangling over the sides of the wagon; all thirsty, and calling almost incessantly for water."

Many local women brought food to the wounded and attended them as volunteer nurses. Years later, Union surgeon Samuel M. Melcher remembered in particular, for example, Mary Phelps and Dorinda Boyd, wife of Marcus Boyd, as women who helped care for the wounded.

When the defeated Federals straggled into Springfield on the late afternoon of August 11, and it became clear that the Union forces would be retreating to Rolla, most of the remaining townspeople made preparations to leave with the army. Springfield had been predominantly unionist even at the time the war broke out, and it was considerably more so after two months of Federal occupation, many secessionists having fled to other climes. The loyal citizens did not want to be in town when the Confederates reached Springfield, and those who hadn't already prepared for the exodus started hurriedly loading their wagons. Mary Phelps, for instance, loaded up her children and most of her family's slaves in two wagons for the trip to Rolla, while she and one slave stayed behind to help take care of the wounded. Many merchants, some of whom had previously sold their goods to soldiers at inflated prices, now started giving food away or else dumping it into the streets rather than let it fall into the hands of the Confederates.

Private Ware recalled the tumult that he and his Iowa comrades witnessed upon their return to Springfield after the battle:

> *As we came into town, grocery merchants hailed us to come in and get what we wanted. One of our men took a ham, another found something to put some sugar in; some took one thing, some another. One merchant pounded in a sugar hogshead on the street and told the boys to take all of it if they could. It was so with tobacco and nearly everything else. Union men did not want to furnish the rebel army with supplies. Everything was in a hurly-burly, and the officers were all swearing at each other.*

At Springfield on the evening of August 11, Major Sturgis, who had assumed command on the field after Lyon's death, handed the Union army over to Colonel Sigel. All of the officers agreed that the Federals should withdraw promptly, and they made preparations to march during the wee hours of the following morning. It was nearly 4:00 a.m., though, before the head of the immense Federal train started toward Rolla, and the procession, consisting of 370 wagons, was so long that it took two hours before the tail of the column finally inched out of Springfield.

During the haste and confusion of the Federal retreat from the Wilson's Creek battlefield, General Lyon's body had been left behind. The victorious Southerners discovered it and turned it over to Dr. Melcher, who had stayed on the field to treat the wounded. Escorted by a detail of the Missouri State Guard, Melcher brought the body to Springfield the night after the battle. It was placed in the general's former headquarters on College Street, and a group of local women, in keeping with a common mourning custom of the time, sat up with the body the rest of the night. The next day, the decomposing body was taken to the Phelps farm for storage in an icehouse, but Mary Phelps, afraid that Southern soldiers might desecrate the corpse, had it buried in a nearby cornfield on August 13. Arriving in Springfield from the East, relatives of Lyon had the body disinterred on August 23 and escorted it back to Connecticut, where it was finally laid to rest on September 5.

Chapter 5

The Confederates Take Over the Town

The first Southern soldiers to reach Springfield, four companies of the Third Texas Cavalry, rode into town on the morning of August 11, almost twenty-four hours after the Battle of Wilson's Creek had ended. Finding the town largely abandoned except for wounded Union soldiers and the surgeons who had stayed behind to treat them, the cavalrymen tore down the U.S. flag at the courthouse, ripped it to pieces, and triumphantly hoisted a Confederate banner to take its place.

Most citizens of Springfield had departed with the Union army, and some of the ones who had stayed behind were Southern sympathizers who now left town to go out and greet the victorious Rebels. Few women, in particular, remained in Springfield after the Federal exodus. Writing to his wife from Springfield a few days later, an Arkansas soldier, Captain Harris Flanagin, estimated that there were no more than twenty women in the entire town.

The absence of townspeople made Springfield an easy target for looters, and some of the Southern soldiers, who continued to arrive during the day, fanned out through the town to plunder. Some of the pillagers may have been Springfieldians who had left their homes to join the Missouri State Guard and who were now taking revenge for damage done to their own property by the Union soldiers who had lately occupied the town. Flanagin told his wife that his Arkansas comrades treated the Union citizens of Springfield much better than the Missourians did.

Southern soldiers swamped the few stores that remained open, and thousands of dollars of merchandise changed hands in a short time. Everything was duly paid for, county historian Holcombe noted wryly, "*in Confederate or Missouri scrip.*"

For the most part, however, Springfield had already been pretty well cleaned out before the Rebels arrived. O.A. Williams, assistant surgeon general of the Missouri State Guard, complained upon reaching town that there was "nothing to drink" and "little to eat" in Springfield.

Price and McCulloch visited Springfield sometime on the eleventh and used the time to lay out encampments around the town and make preparations for a long-term occupation. Although it was a Sunday, McCulloch reportedly remarked that it was "just as good as any other day in war time."

On Monday, August 12, Rebel soldiers continued to troop into Springfield, and the town stirred with renewed activity. Well-wishers and

A view of Springfield as it appeared near the time of the Civil War. Springfield, Missouri, #00652, in the collection of Wilson's Creek National Battlefield. *Courtesy of National Park Service.*

prospective recruits flocked to town from the surrounding area to greet the victorious soldiers, and the Southerners raised a Confederate flag in celebration. Captain John Wyatt, a surgeon in the Missouri State Guard, wrote that he visited the "celebrated town" of Springfield for the first time on the twelfth and found it "crowded with soldiers and citizens. The flag of the Confederacy was raised amidst the wildest enthusiasm by all the people. Everyone seemed wild with joy except a few sad faced Dutch who had been left behind by their army. They looked as if they thought their last day had come." (The ceremony witnessed by Dr. Wyatt was presumably a more formal follow-up to the spontaneous flag-raising that the cavalry detachment had carried out the previous morning.)

On or about August 12, most of the Rebel wounded who required hospitalization were moved into Springfield, where they joined the fallen Union soldiers in overcrowded, makeshift hospitals. Quarters to accommodate all the wounded and medicine to treat them became even scarcer, and according to at least one Union report, the Southerners received preferential treatment. Dr. Franklin stated years after the war, for instance, that General Rains confiscated almost all the Union medical supplies shortly after the Rebels entered Springfield, leaving the Union surgeons with barely enough to treat the wounded Federal soldiers for one week. Dr. Melcher, on the other hand, recalled that the Union wounded were generally treated well not only by the Rebel army but also by the citizens of Springfield, even some who were ardent Southern sympathizers.

It is fair to say, though, that the large number of wounded soldiers at Springfield overwhelmed the efforts of both Union and Confederate surgeons. "Springfield presents a rather gloomy appearance," wrote Dr. Williams shortly after the Southern forces had taken possession of the town. "Every house has been converted into a Hospital."

One of the homes that had been pressed into service was that of Louisa Campbell, located on the southern outskirts of town near the corner of Jefferson and Grand. Mrs. Campbell's twelve-year-old granddaughter, Louisa Cheairs McKinney, spent the day of the Wilson's Creek battle at a relative's farm outside Springfield, but the next day, she returned to her grandmother's house and found that the Campbell home had been turned into a hospital. "I do not know how many men we had," she wrote years later, "but there were cots and pallets everywhere filled with Union and Confederate men, many of whom were past all aid. I was given my duties at once. It was no time for anyone to be spared on the score of youth."

Although Dr. Williams claimed that the wounded under his care were generally well, he added that he had performed so many amputations he had become "sick and tired" of taking off arms and legs. A surgeon for an Arkansas unit painted an equally gloomy picture. Writing from Springfield on August 17, Dr. William A. Cantrell said he had "seen and heard nothing but gunshot wounds and the groans of the dying and distressed" during the previous week and that, of the estimated 1,500 to 2,000 combined total of Union and Confederate wounded, many were "receiving poor attention and the greater portion no attention at all."

Writing to his hometown newspaper in Emporia, Kansas, a few days after the Battle of Wilson's Creek, twenty-year-old John B. Clark Jr., who was among the Federal wounded left behind in Springfield, remarked, "You can have no conception of how things look here at this time." The stench of the dead and dying, Clark added, was so terrible as to be almost unbearable.

On August 12, General McCulloch issued a congratulatory order to his men commending them on their victory and admonishing them not to tarnish its glory by committing outrages on the private property of citizens. About the same time, he also issued a proclamation to the people of Missouri. Adopting a more magnanimous attitude toward unionists than Lyon had done toward secessionists, McCulloch promised:

> *I do not come among you to make war upon any of your people, whether Union or otherwise. The Union people will be protected in their rights and property. It is earnestly recommended to them that they return to their homes. Prisoners of the Union party who have been arrested by the army will be released and allowed to return to their friends. Missouri must be allowed to choose her own destiny; no oaths binding your consciences will be administered. I have driven the enemy from among you. The time has now arrived for the people of the State to act; you cannot longer procrastinate. Missouri must now take her position, be it North or South.*

General Ben McCulloch and his Confederate troops occupied Springfield after the Battle of Wilson's Creek. General Ben McCulloch, #31413, in the collection of Wilson's Creek National Battlefield. *Courtesy of National Park Service.*

Despite McCulloch's order to his men and his promise to citizens to protect their rights and property, occasional abuses occurred. As was the case when the Union had held Springfield, the fact that ample food and other provisions to supply an occupying army were not readily available through official channels doubtlessly contributed to the transgressions. "We were in hopes," noted one Southern soldier upon reaching Springfield, "that when we got here we would find the necessaries of life more plenty, but the Dutch were before us."

The Rebels, therefore, foraged throughout Greene County for grain and other foodstuffs to supply their needs, and they sometimes "pressed" the animals and other property of private citizens into the service of the South. Sometimes the sympathies of the owner mattered little, but unionists were particularly singled out. Margaret Gilmore Kelso, who grew up on a farm northwest of Springfield and whose father was a staunch Union man, recalled years later that two men came to her home while Price occupied Springfield, went to the barn lot, and "caught a horse we all loved. He was a fine dapple gray that we called Old Jim. The horse seemed to sense something was wrong and snorted and ran around the lot several times before they finally caught him. How we children hated to see Old Jim go."

Outbreaks of wanton pillaging occasionally occurred as well. "The Southern troops," Private Clark told the readers of the *Emporia News*, "are destroying a great deal of property."

In addition, Union men were sometimes arrested or mistreated only because of their uncompromising loyalty. Former members of Phelps's home guard regiment, although few remained in the Springfield area, were particularly targeted for ill treatment.

General Price established his headquarters in a house on Boonville Street north of Jordan Creek, while General McCulloch set up his center of operations at the Smith Tavern and Hotel just off the square on the east side of Boonville. Both officers entertained a steady stream of civilian visitors, who flocked to their headquarters on business or merely to get a glimpse of the noted generals.

Sterling Price also occupied Springfield with his Missouri State Guard after Wilson's Creek, and he later established a Confederate recruiting camp at Springfield. General Sterling Price, #31505, in the collection of Wilson's Creek National Battlefield. *Courtesy of National Park Service.*

The Southern soldiers, meanwhile, were camped throughout Springfield and on the outskirts of town. Some were at the Fulbright Spring, some farther west, some north of Jordan in the vicinity of Price's headquarters, and some on the Phelps farm south of town. The men, like their commanders, were visited by civilians on a regular basis.

At first, most of the visitors were Southern sympathizers from the immediate Springfield area who merely wanted to congratulate the victorious soldiers or wish them well, but after a few days elapsed and word of the Battle of Wilson's Creek reached the far corners of Missouri and surrounding states, relatives of the soldiers from more distant locales trekked into town to reunite with loved ones. Richard H. Musser, a judge advocate general in Price's army, for instance, recalled years later, "Ladies whose husbands, fathers, and brothers were in the service…began to arrive and gave social life and enjoyment to the society of Springfield."

Relatives of some of the wounded Union soldiers also made the trip to Springfield to be by the side of their hospitalized loved ones. Even some people with no blood relation to any of the soldiers arrived as angels of mercy from surrounding towns and states to help care for the wounded. When word reached Lawrence, Kansas, for instance, that several local men had been killed or wounded at Wilson's Creek, two citizens from Lawrence left almost immediately for Springfield, motivated only by their respect and concern for the victims. Doctors and other medical personnel also came to Springfield to help the overworked military surgeons who had been treating the wounded since the battle.

After several days in Springfield, McCulloch moved his Confederate troops to Pond Spring west of town, the same area where Union soldiers had camped only weeks before. About the same time, Pearce's troops retreated to Arkansas, and a few days later, the Missouri State Guard also began leaving Springfield. Some departed as early as August 22, and most of the rest followed within the next three days. Leaving behind about five hundred men under Colonel Theodore T. Taylor, Price struck for northern Missouri, where the state troops laid siege to Lexington in late September in an effort to break the Union's stronghold on the Missouri River.

Before the last of Price's Missouri troops had marched north, McCulloch withdrew to the Marionville area of Lawrence County. A few days later, however, he sent a detachment under Captain Flanagin back to Springfield to protect the wounded left at the hospital and to guard the town. On Sunday, September 1, Flanagin attended church services in Springfield but found that the spiritual bonds of the town, like every other aspect of everyday life, had been disrupted by the war. Flanagin went to the Baptist church, the only one in town not completely full of wounded men, where he heard Reverend B. McCord Roberts "preach a very good sermon," but Flanagin estimated that not more than twenty citizens were in attendance.

By the first part of September, many of the Federal wounded were being released to return home. About one hundred were discharged on September 2 alone. The rest were reported as doing well at that time, although a few Union soldiers remained hospitalized in Springfield for two or three more months.

Meanwhile, an outbreak of typhoid fever struck the Southern hospital at the Bailey House about the first of September, and fifteen or twenty men reportedly died in a single day. Many of the hospitalized Confederates were moved to Bentonville, Arkansas, about this time.

After ten days in Springfield, Flanagin rejoined McCulloch in Lawrence County, leaving only Taylor's detachment to guard Springfield. During his brief reign, Colonel Taylor caused a number of Union men in the Springfield area to be arrested on charges of giving aid and comfort to the enemy, but most of them were released without being imprisoned. Taylor treated the Federal soldiers who remained hospitalized at Springfield fairly, and years later he was remembered favorably by some of the Union men and their doctors, notably Dr. Melcher, the surgeon.

Although Taylor treated the hospitalized Union soldiers with compassion, the foraging and "pressing" of private property continued under his command, and Union citizens from Springfield and Greene County continued their exodus from the region. A St. Louis newspaperman estimated in mid-September that there were more than one thousand loyal citizens at St. Louis and Rolla who had been driven from southwest Missouri by the Southerners. The Rebels had reportedly "taken everything eatable, drinkable or portable," and the clothing, provisions and valuables of the unionist refugees had been "unceremoniously appropriated" before they were forced to flee. "The wives and families left behind are on *the point of starvation*, being reduced to the necessity of picking up the refuse of the soldiers or asking alms of the secessionists, whose jeers and taunts are more intolerable than the destitution."

Meanwhile, the Confederate flag continued to waft in the breeze, according to Holcombe's history, "unchallenged and undisturbed" at the county courthouse on the Springfield square.

Chapter 6

Zagonyi's Charge

Under pressure from Washington to act against the Southern troops in Missouri, and still stinging from criticism over his failure to reinforce Lyon before the Battle of Wilson's Creek, General Fremont determined in mid-September to operate against Price by first retaking Springfield. It, Fremont declared, was a "strategical point" and "the key to the whole southwestern part of Missouri, commanding an area of nearly 60,000 square miles." Noting the largely loyal population of the region, many of whom had been driven from their homes and were eager to return, Fremont added that not only military strategy, "but a wise and humane policy, demands the reoccupation of that place." (General Lorenzo Thomas, U.S. Army adjutant general, was among the critics who asked pointedly why the idea of Springfield's strategic significance had not occurred to Fremont before the Battle of Wilson's Creek.)

Fremont proposed a coordinated movement of several Federal forces toward Springfield. Sigel and other Union commanders would gather their men in the vicinity of Jefferson City and start south from that area. General David Hunter was ordered to move his division to Rolla, where he would wait until the forces in north Missouri had crossed the Osage River, and then he would start toward Springfield as well. In addition, General James H. Lane from Fort Scott would effect a junction with Major Sturgis near Kansas City, and their combined force would join the expedition.

Former presidential candidate General John C. Fremont marched to Springfield with a forty-thousand-man army in the fall of 1861. General John C. Fremont, #11457, in the collection of Wilson's Creek National Battlefield. *Courtesy of National Park Service.*

After a three-day siege, General Price and the Missouri State Guard troops occupied Lexington on September 20, and the Union defeat forced Fremont to revise his strategy. To counter Price's presence on the Missouri River, Fremont ordered Hunter to Jefferson City to unite with the other Union forces in central Missouri, and the concentration of Federal forces compelled the state guard to retreat to the southwest corner of the state.

However, the Union defeat at Lexington now stood as a fresh blemish on Fremont's diminishing military reputation, and he came under increased pressure to drive Price from the state. Told by President Lincoln to "repair the disaster at Lexington without loss of time," Fremont soon boarded a train to Jefferson City, where he personally joined the troops in the field in the central part of the state. With Price retreating southward, Fremont resolved once again to occupy Springfield as a first step in eliminating the threat of the state guard troops in Missouri.

By early October, Fremont had an army of nearly forty thousand men arrayed to operate against the Southern forces, and the march toward Springfield began near the middle of the month. After a brief delay in crossing the Osage at Warsaw, Fremont and his support force reached Hickory County on October 24 and camped that evening on a farm about six miles south of Quincy. The units accompanying Fremont included Major John Holman's Battalion of Sharpshooters, Lieutenant Colonel L.H. Marshall's regiment of Benton Cadets, and the general's personal "Body Guard," consisting of three companies of cavalry under the command of Major Charles Zagonyi. Sigel, now a brigadier general, was also camped nearby with his division.

Shortly after arriving at the camp south of Quincy, Zagonyi learned from some civilians who had hastened from Greene County to meet the Federal advance that only about three or four hundred Rebels occupied

Major Charles Zagonyi's famous charge drove the Southern forces out of Springfield in the fall of 1861. Charles Zagonyi, #32031, in the collection of Wilson's Creek National Battlefield. *Courtesy of National Park Service.*

Springfield. The Body Guard had been taunted on the streets of St. Louis as "holiday soldiers" because of their easy duty and fancy uniforms, and the Hungarian-born Zagonyi was eager to prove their mettle. He went at once to Fremont's headquarters and asked permission to march forward and drive the Southerners out of Springfield.

Fremont considered the fifty-mile distance to Springfield too far from camp for Zagonyi to undertake such a mission and at first denied the request. However, when Zagonyi called on him again half an hour later pleading for permission, Fremont relented and granted the request, but he told Zagonyi to unite with Major Frank J. White's Prairie Scouts, who had been sent on a reconnaissance toward Springfield by General Sigel only a short time before.

Zagonyi set out with his Body Guard of about 150 men at about nine o'clock on the night of October 24. Nearly two hours later, Zagonyi overtook Major White and assumed overall command of the mission. White's force consisted of Companies C and L of the First Missouri Cavalry, more commonly called the Prairie Scouts, and one company of Irish Dragoons. The dragoons had been organized at Jefferson City to be attached to the Chicago Irish Brigade then at Lexington, but they were temporarily attached to White's cavalry. The total force under Zagonyi now numbered more than three hundred men.

After forming the junction with White, Zagonyi did not pause again until five o'clock the next morning, when he stopped at a farm for breakfast and a brief rest, having covered about twenty-five miles overnight. When the march resumed an hour and a half later, Major White, who had been ill during the trip, was left at the farmhouse with the understanding that he would follow in a carriage as soon as he was able.

Another five-hour march, covering about seventeen miles, brought the Federals at 11:30 a.m. to within eight miles of Springfield, where they came upon a Missouri State Guard foraging party of six to twelve men. Although Zagonyi captured some of the Southerners, at least one escaped to carry an alarm to Springfield.

In the same area, a local farmer informed Zagonyi that Springfield had been reinforced and that 1,800 to 1,900 Rebels now held the town. Zagonyi sent a messenger back to the Union camp with this intelligence, but resolving to press forward on his own, he asked for reinforcements only as a backup in case he was defeated. General Sigel, who read Zagonyi's dispatch before forwarding it to Fremont, sent a reply to Zagonyi advising him not to attack a force that largely outnumbered his own, but the message did not reach the major in time to forestall such an attack.

Allowing time for a scout that had previously been sent forward to bring back a report, Zagonyi paused awhile longer in the same vicinity eight miles north of Springfield and then resumed the march at a deliberate pace. About 1:00 p.m., the scout returned with information that the Rebels were inexperienced troops who could be expected to run in the face of hard fighting. Zagonyi concluded that if the Southerners did run, they would likely flee to the west or southwest, and he decided to approach Springfield from the west in order to cut off such a retreat. Leaving the Bolivar Road about four or five miles north of Springfield at 2:30 p.m., the Federals took a side road to the west and picked up a civilian guide who led them in a southwesterly direction across the countryside toward the Carthage Road (sometimes called the Greenfield Road).

Meanwhile, Major White had revived enough to follow in a carriage, but when he came to the place where Zagonyi had left the main road, no one was there to guide him, and he continued toward Springfield on the Bolivar Road. Near Springfield, he and his half-dozen escorts were captured by a scouting party of the state guard and taken as prisoners to the Southern camp on the west edge of town. Here White was surrounded by an angry knot of Rebels threatening to kill him, but a state guard officer, supposed to be Captain Wroton, intervened to protect him.

Zagonyi reached the Carthage Road about four miles west of Springfield and followed it toward town a short distance before striking across the countryside again to reach the Mount Vernon Road. On a ridge about three miles outside town, he paused at about 4:00 p.m. to address his men. He told them that the enemy they were about to face numbered not 300 or 400 but close to 1,900. While warning them of the dangerous mission they were about to undertake, he also appealed to their sense of honor, challenging them to prove that they were more than guard duty soldiers. Zagonyi told his men that anyone who was too sick or too fatigued from the hard march to do battle could opt out. Not one man, according to Zagonyi, came forward.

In reality, the number of state guard at Springfield did not approach 1,900 and probably numbered only about 1,000 to 1,200. Colonel Taylor had left Springfield with his force almost a week earlier, and Colonel Julian Frazier had just arrived with about 1,000 men. Many of them were fresh recruits, carrying only squirrel rifles or shotguns, and some had no arms at all. The Federals, on the other hand, although outnumbered, were well armed. Many carried revolvers and repeating rifles capable of firing six shots without reloading.

The state guard camp was located about a mile west of Springfield on the south side of the Mount Vernon Road (at about the 1700 to 2200 block of present-day West Mount Vernon Street). Having learned not only of Zagonyi's approach but also of his flanking movement, the Southerners knew that his line of attack would bring him right by their camp, and they quickly made preparations to receive him.

The campground measured about three hundred yards from north to south and perhaps twice that length from east to west. The Mount Vernon Road, which bounded the camp on the north, was a broad, well-traveled road, but the road bordering on the south was a narrow lane.

A field sloped from a flat, wooded elevation at the west end of the campground down to the Jordan Creek Valley at the east end, where the narrow lane on the south side of the camp came to a dead end. The eastern portion of the camp was open land except for a cornfield that bordered the Mount Vernon Road about halfway between the woods and the creek and curved in a semicircle toward the stream. There was also a small stand of trees adjoining the south side of the cornfield. The camp was surrounded by a high rail fence, and a fence also lined the other side of the narrow lane so that the lane was enclosed on both sides. A north–south lane just beyond the woods at the west edge of the camp connected the east–west lane and the Mount Vernon Road. West of this second lane, enclosed by a high board fence, lay the Springfield fairgrounds, where the Rebel train was stationed.

Thick with undergrowth and vines, the dense woods at the top of the hill were impenetrable to riders on horseback, and the state guard concealed marksmen in the brush on either side of the east–west lane where it passed through the woods. A few sharpshooters also lined the lane behind trees or other concealment beyond the woods down the hill. However, most of the infantry, numbering perhaps three hundred, were drawn up just east of the woods in a battle formation that conformed to the tree line and faced southeast toward the lane. The woods behind the Missourians protected their rear and provided cover in case they needed to retreat. Most of the cavalry, about seven hundred strong, were also stationed along the tree line farther north, while some formed out in the open field in front of the small stand of trees facing the lane. In addition, a small detachment of men was posted at the fairgrounds to guard the wagons.

The Body Guard led the Federal column as Zagonyi neared Springfield. Next in the line of march came the Prairie Scouts, followed by the Irish Dragoons. As the Federals neared town, at about 4:30 p.m., Zagonyi paused to address his men a second time. In a brief, fiery speech, he again challenged them to prove that they were more than parade soldiers, and he gave them a battle cry, "Fremont and the Union!" which they were to shout as they charged into the fray.

Having been informed by Union citizens on the Mount Vernon Road that his best line of attack was along the lane bordering the Rebel camp on the south, Zagonyi resumed the march and detoured over to the lane as he approached the fairgrounds. Marching at quick time, the first company of the Body Guard outdistanced the trailing companies, and the command became somewhat separated as the Federals trotted down the lane past the fairgrounds and into the woods. (Contrary to some previous accounts, Zagonyi was already on the narrow east–west lane as he passed the fairgrounds.) As the head of the column emerged from the woods, the Rebels suddenly poured a murderous fire upon the Body Guard that knocked several of them from their saddles and wounded several others. Some of the riderless horses reared and snorted, creating momentary confusion in the ranks, but Zagonyi scarcely hesitated. He saw the forces arrayed against him, but it was too late to turn back now. Seeing the open ground ahead sloping to the creek, he decided that the only thing to do was to run the gauntlet and try to reach the cover of the stream.

With Company A of the Body Guard under Captain Walter Newhall and most of Company B, Zagonyi galloped down the hill under a heavy fire and reached the creek with only a few added casualties. Realizing that the rest of his command had not followed, Zagonyi yelled that they were lost, referring to the detachment at the creek, if the rest of the battalion did not follow, and he waved his saber wildly as a sign for them to come on. His adjutant, Lieutenant Theodore Majthenyi, quickly dismounted and took down the fence north of the lane to gain access to the field, and the Body Guard filed through and formed in a battle line under the shelter of the steep hillside.

Meanwhile, Captain James Foley, commanding Company C of the Body Guard, had paused at the top of the hill near where the lane emerged from the woods. Some of his men dismounted and took down the fence enclosing the Southern camp, and Foley charged the Rebel flank at the edge of the woods. However, a galling fire and a realization that he could not penetrate the thick underbrush drove him back. In Foley's own words, "The men forced their way through a withering fire far enough along the rebel line to discover the hopelessness of attempting to hold the position gained." Foley realized that the Southerners could simply withdraw into the woods, where they were safe from further pursuit by horsemen. Having lost several men killed or wounded in the futile assault, including two lieutenants, Foley now raced down the hill to join Zagonyi, running the gauntlet just as the major had done.

While Foley was taking down the fence and mounting his charge, Captain Charles Fairbanks, commanding Company L of the Prairie Scouts, entered the woods and found the narrow lane crowded with thrashing horses and swarming with the bedlam of battle. At that moment, according to Fairbanks, an unidentified officer of the Body Guard (probably Foley or one of his lieutenants) rode up and told him that some of the Rebels were withdrawing to the north and for him to take the north–south lane that separated the Southern encampment and the fairgrounds to try to cut off their retreat. Fairbanks headed down the lane, followed by Captain Miles Kehoe and Company C of the Prairie Scouts, although a few Prairie Scouts got mixed in with Foley's company and fought with the Body Guard during the rest of the battle.

Bringing up the rear of the Federal column, Captain Patrick Naughton, with his Irish Dragoons, came galloping up behind the Prairie Scouts and were about to follow them when a straggling soldier of the Body Guard pointed in the direction Zagonyi had gone. Forced to choose between staying with the command to which he was temporarily attached or following the Body Guard, Naughton chose the latter and continued down the east–west lane through the woods, but when he reached the point where Foley had taken down the fence, he saw no sign of the other Federals. Assuming that the Body Guard had gone through the opening, Naughton determined to follow.

By now, all the remnants of the Body Guard had formed along the stream under the shelter of the steep slope at the bottom of the hill. In running the gauntlet through the woods and down the hill, about 40 of the guard had been killed, wounded, unhorsed, or otherwise separated from the main body so that the force gathered at the creek now numbered only about 110 men. Part of them formed on the right under Lieutenant Majthenyi and charged the Rebel cavalry stationed at the cornfield and the grove of trees that fronted it. The rest of the command formed on the left and, with Zagonyi personally leading the way, marched up the steep hillside toward the Rebel infantry that lined the main woods.

The Southern cavalry broke and ran at the first fire from the Federal guns before the Union charge had fairly reached the Rebel line. Some leaped from their horses to seek hiding places in the nearby cornfield or woods and some retreated to the more substantial timber at the west end of the camp, but most galloped for the gate at the northwest corner of the campground, which opened onto the Mount Vernon Road.

Sketch depicting Zagonyi's charge, published in *Harper's Weekly*, November 16, 1861.

With the Rebel cavalry on the Union right already flying in every direction, Zagonyi advanced up the hill on the left side of the field. Attaining leveler ground, he ordered an all-out charge on the state guard infantry at the edge of the woods, and the small band of Federals went screaming forward, fanning out as they charged so as to give themselves room to wield their pistols and sabers. The Rebel infantry stood their ground at first, and the fighting became furious, hand-to-hand combat. According to Captain Foley, four men of his company fell near the Rebel flagstaff so close together that a single army blanket could have covered all four of them. Indeed, the fighting was "too desperate to be of long duration," and the Rebel infantry, like their mounted compatriots, soon broke and retreated headlong into the woods, although a few of the braver souls paused long enough to take potshots at the Federals from behind trees. Seeing the Rebel infantry retire into the safety of the woods, Zagonyi now turned his attention to the other side of the field, where he joined in pursuit of the fleeing Southern cavalry.

Zagonyi had just withdrawn from his engagement with the Rebel infantry and was in hot pursuit of their cavalry when Captain Naughton and his Irish Dragoons started through the opening that Foley had made in the fence along the lane close to the woods. Seeing some of the Missouri State Guard infantry still amassed at the edge of the timber, Naughton, in his own words, "charged straight into the camp" and "vigorously engaged" the Southern foot soldiers. Almost immediately, Naughton was shot in the arm and chest, wounding him severely, and his first lieutenant, Patrick Connelly, was mortally wounded with two bullets to the chest. Sergeant McDonnell of the dragoons quickly returned fire, killing one of the sharpshooters who had wounded Connelly. The other Rebel marksman, according to one postwar account, was a fifteen-year-old lad named Johnnie Wickersham.

Both commissioned officers being disabled, Orderly Sergeant Gerrity assumed command and led two more charges that "cleaned out the camp" of the Rebels. After withdrawing into the woods, many of the Southern soldiers began scaling the fences surrounding the campground and fleeing in all directions. Meanwhile, the dragoons took possession of the ground as the Southerners retired.

On the other side of the field, the Body Guard charged into the cornfield after the Rebel cavalrymen who had sought refuge there, rousting them from

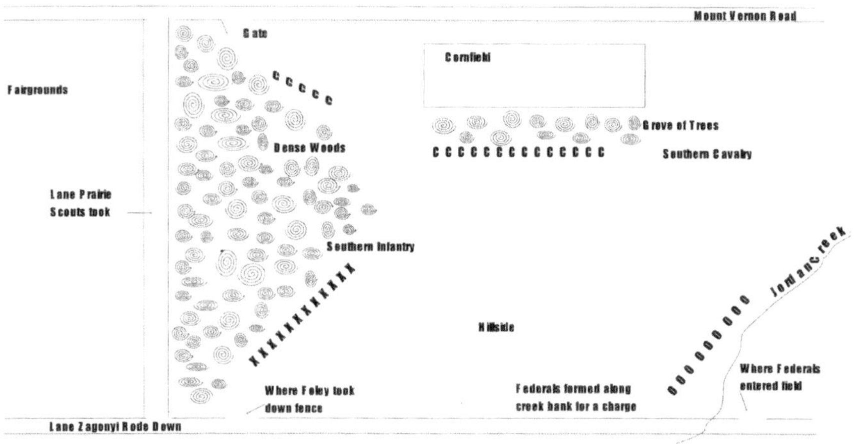

Map of the ground on which Zagonyi's charge took place, based on a map sketched by Major William Dorsheimer that appeared in the February 1862 *Atlantic Monthly*.

their hiding places and shooting them or striking them down with sabers. The Missourians who had stayed in the saddle were pursued across the field and out onto the Mount Vernon Road, where they fled in every direction. The Body Guard chased the fleeing Rebels, horseman and infantrymen alike, into the countryside and through the streets of Springfield, attacking small parties of them wherever they overtook them. According to Major Zagonyi, the Southern soldiers fought harder and did the Federals more harm during these "single-handed attacks, fighting here and there on their own hook," than they did during "their grand first attack."

Zagonyi singled out a Southern lieutenant, in particular, for his bravery. The Rebel officer met Zagonyi and a large party of the Body Guard in a narrow lane and charged right through the Federal line with his pistol blazing. As he brushed past Zagonyi, he placed the barrel of the revolver against the major's side and pulled the trigger, but his galloping horse caused the shot to pass behind Zagonyi, after which one of the Body Guard cut the Rebel down with a saber while another shot him dead. Zagonyi claimed later that, because of the Southern officer's bravery, he "felt some pity to kill him."

The Prairie Scouts, who had made their meandering way around the Southern campground, joined in the rout of the fleeing Rebels.

According to Major White, his men "charged at three different times upon the main body of rebels, with whom I was, as they retreated from one position to another."

All told, Zagonyi "rallied and charged through the streets in all directions about twenty times, clearing the town and neighborhood." During one of the Body Guard's sashays through the streets, John A. Stephens, a local schoolmaster who had watched the battle west of town from atop the courthouse and was headed home, was shot and killed in front of his own house when he ignored an order from a member of the Guards to halt.

Despite the unfortunate killing of Mr. Stephens, the Union citizens of Springfield greeted Zagonyi and his men as deliverers. "As we dashed through the streets," recalled Zagonyi, "the women came out from their houses to the gates of their gardens; waved their handkerchiefs, and brought out flags." Captain Foley, who exchanged words with some of the well-wishers, called the reception that the Federals were accorded in Springfield "an enthusiastic demonstration of long-repressed loyalty and joy over unexpected deliverance."

After charging back and forth several times to rid the streets of Rebels, Zagonyi regrouped on the square and found that he now had only about seventy mounted men, the rest having been killed, wounded, or unhorsed or having gone missing. Upon taking possession of the square, Zagonyi liberated the Union prisoners being held there, detailed pickets to guard the main streets, and raised a Union flag at the courthouse. (After the war, Dr. Melcher disputed the claim that Zagonyi raised a flag at the courthouse, but the contemporaneous evidence suggests that he did.)

Fearful that the Missourians might reunite and return in overwhelming numbers, Zagonyi decided that he "did not want to run the risk of sacrificing the remainder of my men." Therefore, leaving only about twenty horseless men to collect the dead and tend to the wounded, Zagonyi ordered out the local home guard and started back toward Bolivar with the bulk of his command, having held Springfield only a couple of hours. Some of the men left behind also straggled back toward Bolivar as soon as they got a chance.

Meanwhile, the party of Rebels who held Major White prisoner took him with them as they fled Springfield and retreated south into Christian

County, where they stopped to spend the night at the farm of David A. Dryden, a strong Union man. White managed a secret audience with Dryden and told him that he was being held captive. During the night, Dryden dispatched his son to neighboring houses, and soon a group of about twenty home guards had been raised. The Union men reached Dryden's home at about daylight on October 26, liberated Major White, and turned his captors into captives. White then took charge of the party and escorted the prisoners back to Springfield, where he found Dr. Melcher, who had remained in Springfield after Wilson's Creek, and the surgeon of his own Prairie Scouts treating the wounded from the previous day's battle. Otherwise, the town was abandoned except for a few stragglers from the Body Guard and the Prairie Scouts. Seeing that Springfield was virtually deserted and knowing that the Missouri State Guard was still in force in the area, the home guards did not tarry in town but returned quickly to their homes in Christian County. Major White, meanwhile, gathered up the Federal stragglers and found that he had a total of twenty-four men. After posting pickets around the town, he was left with "a reserve of two men."

At about noon, two Missouri State Guard surgeons came into town under a flag of truce requesting to make arrangements to bury the Southern dead. White received them "with as much ceremony as I could muster, and impressed the bearers with an idea that we had a large force, under the dread command of General Sigel, on the outskirts of the village." White then detailed a few of his men to oversee the burial of the dead Southern soldiers that had not already been interred or carried away. Sigel was, in fact, still about forty miles north of town at the time, but White's bluff apparently worked, as the Southerners did not try to attack the small force at Springfield.

Although Zagonyi's charge was an obvious Union victory, casualties were probably about the same on both sides. Zagonyi reported fifteen men of the Body Guard killed, twenty-seven wounded, and ten missing, for a total of fifty-two casualties. Major White reported thirty-three total casualties among the Prairie Scouts but did not specify the number killed, wounded, or missing. Captain Naughton reported two killed and twelve wounded from his company, making a total of about ninety-nine Union casualties.

The loss of the Missouri State Guard is more difficult to determine. One Union report suggested that the Southerners lost 116 men killed alone. Major Zagonyi—based on statements from prisoners, scouts, and civilians—put the number of enemy dead at 106. These estimates, however, are almost surely exaggerated, since both sides during the Civil War tended to inflate the casualties of the enemy while downplaying their own losses. For instance, Moses J. Bradford, a Southern soldier, writing to his wife and mother shortly after Zagonyi's charge, claimed that members of the state guard "killed and wounded 150 of the invaders with the loss of four men." While Bradford might have meant that his unit, not the entire Southern force, lost four men, the statement was still clearly an exaggeration, just as the Union estimates were almost certainly overstatements.

The importance to the Union of the victory at Springfield on October 25, 1861, however, cannot be measured in terms of casualties alone. After the disappointments of Carthage, Wilson's Creek, and Lexington, Zagonyi's intrepid charge and the rout of the Southern soldiers provided a needed boost to the morale of Federal military forces in Missouri, as well as to Union citizens of the state.

Chapter 7

The Federals Reoccupy Springfield

Fremont's advance, consisting of Holman's Sharpshooters, reached Springfield on the morning of October 27. General Sigel's command came in about noon, and Fremont, accompanied by the Body Guard and the Benton Cadets, reached town later the same day. Major William Dorsheimer, an aide-de-camp on Fremont's staff, described the scene as the latter party marched into town:

> *It was a gala-day in Springfield. The Stars and Stripes were flying from windows and house-tops, and ladies and children, with little flags in their hands, stood on the door-steps to welcome us. This is the prettiest town I have found in Missouri, and we can see the remains of former thrift and comfort worthy a village in the Valley of the Merrimack or Genesee. It has suffered severely from the war…War's dreary record is written upon the dismantled houses, the wasted gardens, the empty storehouses, and the deserted taverns.*

In a letter to his mother a few days later, Henry Voelkner, a private in Fremont's army, remarked on the devastation at Springfield in similar terms as Major Dorsheimer: "Springfield must have been a pretty place, but now presents a sorry sight…The houses are largely destroyed or totally forsaken. The stores are plundered and other houses are burned down, etc."

Upon their arrival in Springfield on the twenty-seventh, the Federals accompanying Fremont made their camp at the Phelps farm. The men pitched their tents in the front and side yards of the house, but because the supply wagons had not yet reached town, they were compelled to forage for their supper. Meanwhile, many of the officers were fed and given places to sleep at nearby homes.

That night, the joyous mood that had attended the Federals' arrival was broken when a man who had been arrested earlier in the day while hurrahing for Jeff Davis and confined as a prisoner at the old courthouse in the center of the square set fire to the structure; the building was quickly engulfed in flames. Described as "a crazy old man, well known here, and previously thought to be harmless," the arsonist reportedly clapped his hands in celebration as the flames went up.

In a propitious sign for the Union, as the fire raged, it burned off the halyards of the flagstaff, and Old Glory floated away from the building and landed safely on the ground, only slightly singed. The next day, however, the charred edifice stood, according to Dorsheimer, as "a black ruin, a type of desolation which broods over the once happy and prosperous town."

On October 28, a funeral service for the members of the Body Guard killed in Zagonyi's charge was held at 1:00 p.m. on the public square. They were buried with military honors at the city cemetery, located in the northeast quadrant of State and Campbell Streets,

The Springfield square as it appeared in the fall of 1861, sketched by Alexander Simplot and published in *Harper's Weekly*. Note the old courthouse in the center of the square that had burned just days earlier.

Funeral service on the Springfield square for members of Fremont's Body Guard killed in Zagonyi's charge. Funeral Fremont's Body Guard, #30842, in the collection of Wilson's Creek National Battlefield. *Courtesy of National Park Service.*

and a group of local Union women walked beside the procession to the common grave. Ironically enough, the cemetery plot had been donated to the city by John Stephens, the citizen who was killed by one of Zagonyi's men.

The same day as the funeral, Zagonyi wrote his official report of the action that had occurred three days prior. When the report was made public, it caused what newspaperman Franc Wilkie, accompanying the Federals as he had during the Lyon campaign, called "a small imbroglio" between Zagonyi and the officers whose commands had been temporarily attached to the Body Guard. Zagonyi spoke of his own men in glowing terms, and he and the Body Guard were hailed as heroes in the Union press during the days following their daring charge. On the other hand, Zagonyi cast the Prairie Scouts and the Irish Dragoons in an unfavorable light, suggesting that they had abandoned him in the heat of battle.

A day or two later, Major White learned that a group of Union ladies of Springfield planned to present a flag to the Body Guard in recognition of its gallant charge and its recapture of the town. Indignant over the

Major Frank White, who disputed the claim that his Prairie Scouts had not behaved gallantly during Zagonyi's charge. Major Frank White, #11762, in the collection of Wilson's Creek National Battlefield. *Courtesy of National Park Service.*

imputation of cowardice contained in Zagonyi's report, White persuaded the women that he and the Prairie Scouts were also entitled to receive such a banner, and the ladies agreed to make the presentation. On November 1, he and his command rode formally up to Worrell's store on the south side of the square, where the storeowner's wife, Mrs. Sophia Worrell, and several other women gave Major White a flag, and he responded, according to Wilkie, with a "neat and appropriate speech."

Just as the little ceremony was concluding, Zagonyi, according to Holcombe's county history, rode onto the square, saw the Prairie Scouts leaving with their flag, and promptly returned to his quarters, "purpling the air with Hungarian profanity." The ladies wanted to go ahead with their presentation of a flag to the Body Guard, but the fiery and petulant Zagonyi sent them a letter on November 2 declining the offer because the same distinction had already been accorded to a body of men who "deserted me at the very moment of conflict, and exposed the officers and men of the Body Guard to a fate which the hand of Providence alone could avert."

Zagonyi's report particularly incensed Captain Naughton, who claimed that, regardless of whether the insinuation of cowardice might rightly apply to the Prairie Scouts, it most certainly did not apply to the Irish Dragoons. Naughton demanded and received a military board of inquiry into the charges contained in Zagonyi's report, and the board exonerated the Irish Dragoons and, for the most part, the Prairie Scouts as well. Zagonyi, however, declined to amend his official report, and Naughton continued, through military channels and in open letters to St. Louis newspapers, to press for an apology or an explanation. Although none was forthcoming, both the Scouts and the Dragoons eventually received a measure of recognition for their part in Zagonyi's celebrated charge.

After the Siege of Lexington, the Missouri State Guard retreated to the southwest corner of Missouri. Price was still amassing his forces there in late October when Governor Jackson's legislature met in exile at Neosho and passed a secession bill on the twenty-eighth that, at least in the eyes of Southern sympathizers, took the state out of the Union. Having learned of the Federals' reoccupation of Springfield, Union refugees from southwest Missouri once again flocked into town, bringing complaints of depredations by the Rebel soldiers and extravagant claims about the strength of Price's army. When Jackson moved his rump government to Cassville during the last days of October, and the state guard forces accompanied him, bringing them nearer to Greene County, a mild panic coursed through Springfield, since all of Fremont's forces had not yet arrived. For a time, a second great battle, similar to Wilson's Creek and perhaps on the same ground where it had been fought, was thought inevitable.

Frightened Union citizens were not the only refugees flocking into Springfield. Without authority from Washington, General Fremont had issued an "emancipation proclamation" on September 30 freeing Missouri's slaves, and many runaway blacks poured into town seeking the protection of the Federal army. Many of the officers in Fremont's volunteer units were abolitionists who welcomed the blacks, and they put them to work performing various tasks about camp. Most of the officers of the regular army had "little sympathy with this practical Abolitionism," according to Major Dorsheimer, but it was different with the rank and file soldiers. Anticipating what few people in the United States had yet come to realize—that the Civil War was to be a war for emancipation—Dorsheimer said that, although the average soldiers might not have thought very deeply about the social and legal questions surrounding slavery, they were abolitionists by the inescapable logic of their circumstance. "Is it to be supposed," he asked pointedly, "that men who, like the soldiers of the Guard, last week pursued Rebellion into the very valley and shadow of death, will be solicitous to protect the system which incited their enemies to that fearful struggle, and hurried their comrades to early graves?"

In some cases, the owners of runaway slaves came to Springfield seeking the return of their "property" and were unceremoniously turned away. Dorsheimer cited the example of a farmer who came into the Federal lines inquiring about his slave and was directed to Colonel Owen Lovejoy, who had employed the runaway as a paid servant. Lovejoy, an ardent abolitionist and a U.S. congressman from Illinois who was accompanying the Federal army as a member of Fremont's staff, brusquely dismissed the farmer when he called at the colonel's headquarters. "That man is my servant," proclaimed Lovejoy. "By his own consent he is in my service, and I pay him for his labor…Do you dare come here and claim the person of my servant? He is entitled to my protection, and shall have it. I advise you to leave this camp forthwith."

Some of the blacks in Springfield did not arrive as runaways but instead were already servants attached to the Federal army before Fremont occupied the town. Some blacks even arrived as soldiers, notably those under the command of Kansas senator and rabid abolitionist Jim Lane. On October 30, General Alexander Asboth's division reached Springfield, followed later the same day by Lane's brigade, which, according to Dorsheimer, was "a motley procession, made up of the desperate fighters of the Kansas borders and about two hundred negroes. The contrabands were mounted and armed, and rode through the streets rolling about in their saddles with their shiny faces on a broad grin."

The Federals' second occupation of Springfield would prove to be brief, and the amount of plundering and destruction of civilian property was minimal during the short stay. Holcombe's county history, while suggesting that Fremont's large army not unexpectedly included a few "lawless characters…who would steal anything from a negro to a spring pullet," allowed that there was very little "open pillaging." Lane's Kansans, who were particularly notorious for stealing property and "liberating" blacks, did, however, carry off a number of Greene County slaves, including some who had belonged to Union men. The large size of Fremont's army also necessitated foraging throughout the orchards and cornfields of Greene County, but whenever property was taken from Union citizens, they were given vouchers and, in most cases, eventually received full pay for the property.

Although the Union army did not officially enlist blacks until later in the war, abolitionist Kansas senator Jim Lane had many in his command when he came to Springfield in the fall of 1861. *Courtesy of J. Dale West Collection.*

In fact, Fremont entered into negotiations with Price seeking an agreement that would ensure the rights of all private citizens, regardless of political beliefs. A joint proclamation to the citizens of Missouri was drafted noting that no citizen should be arrested solely because of his political opinion, and the decree also outlawed all bodies of armed men who were not authorized by Fremont or Price or legitimately connected to one of their armies. Fremont signed the agreement on November 1 and forwarded it to Price, but events were already in motion that would make the agreement null and void before it ever took effect.

President Lincoln was not happy with General Fremont over his belated response to the Southern threat in Missouri and his less than vigorous prosecution of the war. He was even more annoyed by the "emancipation proclamation" that Fremont had issued on September 30 freeing Missouri's slaves because the president knew that it would alienate slaveholding Union men in the state. Lincoln preferred a slow-and-steady approach to the emancipation issue.

Rumors of Fremont's removal began filtering into Springfield in late October, but the official word that he had been relieved of duty and was to be replaced by General Hunter did not reach Fremont until the morning of November 2. Although disappointed, he received the news stoically and immediately issued an order transferring the command to Hunter, with General John Pope, who had reached Springfield with his division the day before, to take over until Hunter's arrival. Fremont also drew up an address announcing the change and ordered it to be read to the soldiers of his army. The circulation of Fremont's farewell address, according to Wilkie, created "a profound impression" among the soldiers, especially in the Germans units, where the men of one or two whole companies threw down their arms and declared that they would no longer serve. In addition, several officers offered their resignations, and only the entreaties of General Fremont convinced them to stay.

When Hunter still had not arrived the next day, November 3, and rumors of a concentration of Southern forces near Wilson's Creek continued to reach Springfield, the chief Union officers called at Fremont's office, at the same house on College Street where Lyon had had his headquarters, and beseeched the general to lead the Federal army against Price the next morning if Hunter still had not arrived at that time. Finally consenting, Fremont drew up a battle plan, and when word reached the camps that he had resumed command and would lead the Federals into battle the next morning, the soldiers greeted the news with the "wildest enthusiasm," according to a St. Louis newspaper correspondent.

Late that night, however, Hunter finally arrived with his division and took command, bringing with him orders from the War Department to fall back to Rolla and Sedalia. The thinking in Washington was that the Southern forces in southwest Missouri were little more than a decoy to draw the Federals away from the Mississippi so that the Confederates could make their way up the river and capture St. Louis. This, of course, was the same idea that had caused Fremont to withhold reinforcements from Lyon before the Battle of Wilson's Creek.

Fremont's grand design to march against Price's army dissolved with the arrival of Hunter, who correctly believed that the Southerners were not in force in the neighborhood of Springfield. In fact, only a cavalry force of about 1,500 Rebels was in the vicinity of Wilson's Creek, while the bulk of Price's army was still concentrated in the Cassville area.

Having been relieved of duty, Fremont left Springfield on November 4, the very next day after Hunter's arrival. Led by a small band and accompanied by his Body Guard and the Sharpshooters, he marched out of town "to merry music" at about 9:00 a.m. When the entourage reached St. Louis a few days later, Zagonyi and the Body Guard were mustered out of service, because they were perceived as being too zealously loyal to Fremont, with the battle cry "Fremont and the Union!" that they supposedly yelled during their famous charge at Springfield being cited as evidence against them.

Meanwhile, back in Springfield, General Hunter wrote a letter on November 7 informing General Price that he would not recognize the treaty between Fremont and Price forbidding the arrest of citizens merely for their political opinions and outlawing bodies of armed men not officially affiliated with the Northern or the Southern armies. Among Hunter's reasons for rejecting the agreement was a concern that the latter stipulation might be construed as outlawing home guard units.

Whether Hunter recognized the Price-Fremont agreement hardly mattered, however, since Hunter himself marched out of Springfield on November 9 with his thirty-thousand-man army, leaving southwest Missouri once again in Southern hands. Not caring to trust themselves to the "tender mercies" of the Confederates, hundreds of Union families from Greene and surrounding counties, according to Holcombe's county history, once again set out in advance of or with the Federal army, and the roads were filled for miles with trudging refugees. Many of the citizens of Greene County who left did not come back until after the war, and some did not return at all.

Chapter 8

The Rebels Move Back In

In the face of the overwhelming Federal numbers at Springfield, Price had dropped back from Cassville on November 7 to the Pineville area of McDonald County. A week later, however, General McCulloch, who was camped along the Wire Road near the Arkansas line, got word of the Federal withdrawal, and he started for Springfield on November 16 and camped on the outskirts of town on the night of the eighteenth. The next morning, he came into Springfield and reported to the Confederate secretary of war that the place was "almost deserted," nearly all the Union men having fled with the Federal army. A few Missouri State Guard troops also filtered into Springfield at this time, but most were with Price over seventy miles away.

McCulloch stayed in Springfield only a few days before retreating once again to Arkansas. Meanwhile, Price marched north from the southwest corner of Missouri and set up a recruiting camp at Osceola. It wasn't long, though, before a portion of the state guard poured back into Springfield. General James H. McBride, a former resident of the city, arrived on December 1 with two thousand men, and the rest of the Missouri troops came in later in the month. Price himself arrived on Christmas Day with plans to spend the remainder of the winter. Lemuel Donnell, a state guard lieutenant who reached Springfield a few days after Price, recorded in his diary that he and his company set up their tents "with a deep snow on the ground and very cold."

After the act of secession at Neosho, the promise of a commission as a major general in the Confederate army was dangled in front of Price on the condition that he bring as many of his troops as possible into the Confederate army with him. Most of the Missouri State Guard had enlisted for six months, and their terms were now expiring. Operating out of his old headquarters on Boonville Street, Price therefore spent much of his time in Springfield during December and January recruiting for the Confederacy and reorganizing his command. All told, Price enlisted about four thousand men into Confederate service while he was at Springfield.

Price and his officers also spent a good deal of time drilling and trying to instill discipline in the new Confederate troops. For instance, Captain Emmett MacDonald, commanding MacDonald's Flying Artillery or the St. Louis Battery, issued company orders in late January that there was to be "no loud noise, swearing or drinking allowed in the camp" at Springfield. "All lights in tents to be extinguished at 10 o'clock." MacDonald further decreed

Emmett MacDonald laid down strict rules for his battery of Flying Artillery while the Confederates occupied Springfield during the winter of 1861–62. Colonel Emmett MacDonald, #30826, in the collection of Wilson's Creek National Battlefield. *Courtesy of National Park Service.*

that there were to be two drills daily, at 9:00 a.m. and 2:00 p.m., from which no one would be excused without permission of the captain.

The Southern soldiers were also employed in scouting and foraging throughout the county. Although corn, meat, and other foodstuffs were sometimes confiscated with no pay whatsoever offered to the owner, a species of currency called "Missouri scrip," which had been authorized by Governor Jackson's Neosho legislature and printed shortly afterward, was often tendered. For instance, Margaret Gilmore Kelso, the young girl who lived northwest of Springfield, recalled years later that "a forage train of I don't know how many wagons" pulled up at her father's farm. "They took all the corn we had in the crib and all the hay we had. They also went into the smokehouse and filled one wagon box full of meat… The foragemaster paid mother in Confederate money. It was perfectly worthless, he knew, but he put up a good show of being honest."

Wanton pillaging by the Southern soldiers, however, was minimal. On January 5, 1862, about ten days after his arrival in Springfield, Price issued orders admonishing his command that "no depredations upon property by officers and soldiers of the army occupying houses in and around the city be committed by them or allowed to be committed by others." Fruit and ornamental trees, shrubbery, and fences around yards were not to be injured or destroyed. Having received reports of foraging by freebooters representing themselves as soldiers, Price also issued an order two days later outlawing any foraging not authorized by his command, and the directive required all persons who were neither members of the army nor citizens of Greene County to leave the county unless they had special permission to remain. About the same time, a large Confederate supply train arrived from Arkansas, and the infusion of clothing, camp equipage, and other goods further diminished pillaging and stealing. Price later was pleased to report that he received only a "few complaints" of misconduct while the Southerners held Springfield.

The conduct of the soldiers may have been commendable enough, but Springfield and indeed the entire county, according to Holcombe's history, still "comprised a grand military camp" during the Confederate occupation in the winter of 1861–62. Civil court had been suspended months before, and all legal proceedings were conducted under martial law, with the provost marshal serving as the arbiter of disputes among civilians. Tents and crudely constructed huts dotted the vacant lots of Springfield and the surrounding countryside, and nearly every house or building in town was occupied as a military headquarters, a hospital, a barracks, or a stable. The townspeople were, in Holcombe's words, "compelled to admit that they were living in the Southern Confederacy."

In early February 1862, a correspondent of the *Liberty Tribune* visited the Confederate encampment at Springfield and reported:

> *We were very much gratified to witness the order, neatness, system and comfort which seemed to pervade this camp. Some of the Regiments were on their parade grounds, and a splendid military spectacle it was; the discipline, movement and action of the troops were admirable. We cannot see how a soldier can resist the temptation to join this admirable division of the army.*

By the time the correspondence appeared in the *Tribune* on February 14, however, any prospective enlistee in Price's army could not have enrolled at Springfield. In December 1861, the Union had created the Army of the Southwest, with Brigadier General Samuel R. Curtis in command. Curtis came to the job with orders to push Price out of Missouri, and by late January 1862, he had concentrated an army of about fifteen thousand men at Rolla. He quickly advanced to Lebanon and by early February was marching toward Springfield.

As it turned out, though, Price did not have to be pushed out of Springfield. A mere nudge was sufficient. When he first got word of the Federal advance with a force superior to his own, he appealed to McCulloch and other Confederates in Arkansas for reinforcements, but when none seemed forthcoming, Price started making preparations to vacate Springfield. A detachment of Confederate pickets skirmished with the Federal advance guard east of Springfield near present-day Strafford on February 12, and the Southern soldiers promptly fell back to Springfield. That night, the Confederate withdrawal began in earnest, and a number of families of Southern sympathy packed up and joined the exodus. By the time Curtis reached Springfield at about 10:00 a.m. the next morning, Price and his men were headed down the Cassville Road on their way to Arkansas, where they would join other Confederate forces in fighting and losing the pivotal Battle of Pea Ridge in early March.

Chapter 9

The Union Takes Over Again

The Union people of Springfield who had endured the Confederate occupation turned out to greet the Federal soldiers as they marched into town on the heels of Price's evacuation. Accompanying Curtis's army were a good number of Springfield citizens who were returning home after having received assurances that the Federals would not abandon southwest Missouri again.

The occasion also marked a homecoming for some of the Union soldiers, notably many of those in John S. Phelps's regiment and Pony Boyd's Twenty-fourth Missouri Infantry. The units had recently been organized at Rolla, and they contained many Springfield men who, in some cases, were greeted by loved ones as they marched into town. Robert P. Matthews, a member of the Phelps regiment, recalled:

> *It was an hour of joy. It was an hour of triumph to the Phelps men and the 24th Mo. There is a language of the heart which speaks when all words fail to convey the thought. So with the members of our regiments whose homes and friends were here. When those friends met us, as many of them did, words were useless, the quivering lip and throbbing heart, alone could speak the welcome greetings between those whom grim visage war had separated with the palling clouds of doubt, despair and gloom.*

General Samuel R. Curtis drove the Confederates out of Springfield in February 1862. General Samuel R. Curtis, #31443, in the collection of Wilson's Creek National Battlefield. *Courtesy of National Park Service.*

Upon their arrival in Springfield on February 13, the Federals hoisted a Union flag over the courthouse and took possession of the town. The next day, though, Curtis resumed his pursuit of Price, leaving only a small portion of his army at Springfield, including detachments of the Ninth Iowa Infantry, the Third Iowa Cavalry, and the Twenty-fourth Missouri Infantry. Lieutenant Colonel James K. Mills of the Twenty-fourth Missouri, or the "Lyon Legion" as it was sometimes called, had command of the post. (Colonel Boyd had remained at Rolla in charge of the post there.)

Despite Price's orders to respect the property of private citizens, the Confederates had left Springfield a mess. Hay and straw, which the soldiers had used as bedding, covered the floors of houses. Piles of rubbish lined the streets, and so much filth had accumulated that only the cold of winter prevented the stench from being unbearable. "In nearly every hollow was a cess-pool," according to Holcombe, "and in every alley a muck-heap."

According to some reports, the newcomers contributed to the devastation by burning or otherwise destroying property of Southern sympathizers. Lyman Bennett, a soldier who arrived from Rolla a week after Curtis had passed through Springfield, recorded in his diary, "The place was thronged with soldiers who made free with the property of secesh as if it was theirs." Later he added, "Many buildings, many of them large and elegant, have been burned, some say by our soldiers and others say by the owners themselves who have fled with Price to the South." Among the buildings burned was the house on College Street that Lyon had used as his headquarters before the Battle of Wilson's Creek.

Bennett continued his description of the shambles: "The large stone chimneys common to the country generally remain standing. No place that I have seen tells so fearfully of the dread effects of war as Springfield and its environs, and no picture, however vividly drawn, has ever conveyed to my mind its saddening realities so clearly as the desolation I have seen with my own eyes."

Despite the reports of damage done by some of the Union soldiers when they first got to Springfield, the Federals mainly spent the first two or three weeks clearing streets, cleaning houses, and repairing store buildings. Soon new businesses started springing up, and some of the old ones that had been closed for several months opened back up. The post office reopened, and the mail started running. In early March, a telegraph line connecting Springfield to St. Louis was completed, and shortly afterward it was extended down the Fayetteville Road to Cassville and beyond. A new newspaper, the *Springfield Missourian*, began printing. A steam mill opened and started paying farmers good money for their wheat and corn. The townspeople were paid in U.S. currency for their goods and services, and soon they were able to purchase items that they had done without for so long. On March 2, services were held at the Presbyterian church, supposed to be the first divine services held in Springfield during the year of 1862. In short, a semblance of everyday life began to return to the town.

In addition to the detachments left by Curtis, another military force present at Springfield after the Federals left in pursuit of Price was that of John M. Richardson, who had been commissioned a captain in the budding Missouri State Militia (MSM) and was actively enlisting soldiers for his company, called the Mountain Rangers. Financed by Washington but under the control of Missouri's provisional governor, the Missouri State Militia was created to maintain order in the state and to meet any Rebel threat within Missouri's borders. Richardson and others called a mass meeting at Springfield on March 3, 1862, to discuss the idea of organizing a whole regiment for the Missouri State Militia, drawn from the Union men of southwest Missouri. Many recruits signed up on the spot, and Richardson was later commissioned a colonel of the Fourteenth Cavalry Missouri State Militia, which included three companies composed largely of Greene County men.

When word reached Springfield on March 10 of Curtis's victory at Pea Ridge, the "utmost good feeling and enthusiasm" prevailed, reported a correspondent of the *St. Louis Daily Missouri Republican*, and the townspeople joined the soldiers in celebrating the glorious occasion. "In the absence of cannon, the anvils have been sending forth their thunder notes, the band of the Ninth Iowa has been regaling our ears with the familiar music of the 'Star Spangled Banner' and other National airs, and speeches have been made to an immense crowd." Among the speakers was Marcus Boyd of Springfield.

When the Federals first reached Springfield, the courthouse, the Bailey House, and one church (probably the Methodist church) were being used as hospitals, housing about four hundred sick and wounded Southern soldiers who had been left behind by Price. The convalescing Rebels were required to wear green or yellow stripes on their sleeves as identification. Shortly after the Federals arrived, a general military hospital for Union soldiers was also established at the Daniel D. Berry place in the northeast part of Springfield, and some of the wounded from Pea Ridge were brought there for treatment. (Berry, considered the wealthiest man in southwest Missouri, was a Confederate sympathizer who had gone south at the same time as or shortly after Price's exit.) One wounded soldier brought to Springfield was Albert Demuth, whose family had formerly lived in the town. In early April, he wrote to his parents, now living in Iowa, urging his father to come back to Springfield to find employment. "Business is brisker here now," Demuth told his folks, "than it ever has been since Springfield was a town."

The sight of sick and wounded soldiers being brought into town scarcely dampened the joy occasioned by the news of the Federal victory in Arkansas. The Confederates had been driven entirely out of Missouri and soundly defeated. It was clear that Springfield was to be a major storehouse for the Army of the Southwest, and the town would not likely be abandoned again. The merchants of Springfield transacted business, the townspeople went about their daily lives, and the farmers in outlying areas planted their crops, all with renewed confidence that they would be protected. As Holcombe's county history has suggested, nearly all the citizens of Greene County now claimed to be unionists, whether they were or not, and they entered into an unspoken agreement with the Federal troops by which they would feed and support the soldiers and the soldiers would protect them.

The Federal occupation of Springfield during the spring of 1862 not only revived business activity in the town but also enabled the restoration of civil law. Both the circuit court and the county court convened for the first time in about a year, and many of the warrants issued resulted from the chaos and political divisions spawned by the war. John P. Campbell, nephew of John Polk Campbell, was accused of giving aid and comfort to the enemy and charged by a grand jury in late February with treason for furnishing beef cattle to Price's army during its recent stay in Springfield. (He was later found not guilty.) In May, William A. Campbell, the youngest son of John Polk Campbell, was charged with having stolen cattle the previous September from Lewis Crenshaw, the Union citizen who had served as a guide for Lyon's army before Wilson's Creek.

In late May 1862, General Egbert B. Brown of the Missouri State Militia was appointed commander of the Southwest Division, with headquarters at Springfield. It was increasingly clear that the town was to be a permanent post and a major supply point for the Federal army. Although the number of soldiers assigned to the Springfield garrison in the spring of 1862 was relatively small, varying from about 600 to 1,200, many more passed through on their way to other posts or to reinforce Curtis.

After Pea Ridge, the Confederacy virtually abandoned Missouri, as General Price, whose commission as a major general in the Southern army had been approved, was sent east of the Mississippi. Only fragments of the Missouri State Guard, consisting primarily of men who had balked at

General Egbert B. Brown commanded the forces at Springfield during Marmaduke's invasion of Missouri and attack on Springfield. General E.B. Brown, #31447, in the collection of Wilson's Creek National Battlefield. *Courtesy of National Park Service.*

following Price into Confederate service, remained to carry on the fight for Missouri. Reduced to mere bands, they often resorted to sabotage, marauding, and plundering. Some ex-members of the state guard who had declined to reenlist also took to the bush, and by the early summer of 1862, the Civil War in the state had degenerated into all-out guerrilla warfare. "Bands of murderers, robbers, and other outlaws…professing to act under the authority of the so-called Confederate States," according to General Brown, were making it "almost impossible for peaceful, law abiding citizens, and especially good Union citizens, to pursue their legitimate vocation without molestation and imminent danger."

To counter these outrages, General Brown issued an order on June 6 directing that the members of any band of guerrillas caught committing a crime or otherwise acting against the laws and authority of the United States were to be shot on the spot and that anyone found to be harboring the marauders was to be arrested. When Brown saw, after ten days, that these steps were insufficient to discourage the guerrilla bands, he adopted an even more stringent policy toward civilians. Although the civil courts had been reestablished in Greene County earlier in the year, citizens continued to live under martial law (as they would in one form or another throughout the war), and General Brown ordered that all citizens residing in the Southwest Division of the District of Missouri be required to take the oath of allegiance. Anyone refusing to do so would not only be denied the privileges of citizenship like voting but would not even be allowed to transact business or to be away from his own premises.

Later in the summer, the Enrolled Missouri Militia (EMM) was created as an additional step to combat the guerrilla bands infesting the state. The EMM was to serve as a home guard force to be called up only in emergencies, and it would free up the Missouri State Militia to pursue the guerrillas throughout the state. The stipulation that all able-bodied men not already in military service were required to sign up resulted in the enlistment of many men of questionable loyalty and drove many others into Confederate service. This, however, was not a major problem in Greene County, where two regiments of Enrolled Missouri Militia, the Seventy-second and the Seventy-fourth, were organized under colonels Colley B. Holland and Marcus Boyd.

While most of the outrages in the rural areas of southwest Missouri after the Federal occupation of 1862 were committed by freebooters who identified, at least nominally, with the Southern cause, any crime or atrocity committed in Springfield was more likely authored by the Union soldiers themselves. For example, one of the more notorious incidents of the war occurred on the evening of May 21, 1862, when Captain John R. Clark of the Fifth Kansas Cavalry, who was officer of the day at the Springfield post, got drunk and, in the company of his orderly, A.J. Rice, called at the home of a widow lady named Willis and demanded dinner. Although he had joined a Kansas unit, Clark was a former sheriff of Mercer County, Missouri, and he was considered by some of the men of his own regiment to be a "Pro slavery brute" who "ought to have joined the rebels instead of our side."

Mrs. Willis had recently taken refuge at Springfield to escape the depredations of bushwhackers who had terrorized her family in northern Arkansas. The house on the east side of Springfield where she was placed, according to at least one report, had been previously occupied by "a squad of accommodating girls," and guards had been posted at her home to prevent unwelcome intrusions. When Mrs. Willis refused the demand to prepare a meal, Clark and Rice grew irate, began cursing, and drew their pistols. When they attempted to force their way into the house, one of the two guards shot Clark through the chest, and the captain staggered back a few steps and sank to the ground dead. Rice shot at the guard who had killed Clark but missed and hit Mrs. Willis's daughter, Mary, in the head, killing her instantly. The second guard then shot Rice through the body, mortally wounding him. Clark was buried the next day without military honors.

Despite the devastation of the rural areas around Springfield and despite isolated incidents like the Willis tragedy in the city itself, Springfield overall had begun to prosper by early August 1862 under the Federal occupation. As a Springfield correspondent to the *New York Times* noted in a report entitled "Springfield Today and Springfield a Year Ago," the first year of the war had not been good to the town: "What Ben McCulloch's men commenced, exasperated Unionists completed, and crumbling brick walls and desolated homesteads attest in every direction the avenging power of War. Still, Springfield lives, and, to a certain extent flourishes."

Although Curtis had moved east and established his headquarters at Helena, he remained in Arkansas with his Army of the Southwest throughout the summer of 1862. Defense of Missouri fell largely to the Missouri State Militia, which had been organized only a few months earlier. Militia commander Brigadier General John M. Schofield fretted over how best to protect the state from the roving guerrilla bands or possible invasion from the South with only raw, inexperienced troops at his disposal. The military depot at Springfield, more than one hundred miles removed from the nearest railhead at Rolla and less than seventy miles from Arkansas, was especially vulnerable. When General Brown wired Schofield on August 10 suggesting that he might have to abandon Springfield because of Southern forces that were concentrating near Newtonia in the southwest corner of Missouri, Schofield replied that General Brown should not leave Springfield and advised him instead to entrench his position by building three or four fortifications on the highest points of the city.

Brown wasted no time carrying out the suggestion, as plans were drawn up for five Springfield forts, and construction started in mid- to

John M. Schofield, who was in Springfield as a major prior to Wilson's Creek, later served as a general commanding the Missouri State Militia Cavalry and suggested to General Brown in the summer of 1862 the building of fortifications at Springfield. Major John M. Schofield, #11727, in the collection of Wilson's Creek National Battlefield. *Courtesy of National Park Service.*

late August. In what appears to be the first recorded evidence of work on the defenses, an officer of the Thirty-seventh Illinois Infantry, David Ash, wrote in a letter of August 28, 1862, that he and two fellow officers of the Thirty-seventh had been detached two days earlier for duty overseeing construction of the fortifications, although the initial work might have begun before the twenty-sixth.

Most Civil War forts, including the Springfield forts, did not fit the popular image of rectangular stockades made of tall poles anchored in the ground, with blockhouses at each corner, such as one might conceive from watching old TV westerns. Instead, they were simple earthenworks called redoubts and were not designed to be lived in. A moat or ditch surrounded them, and the dirt taken from the ditch was piled up against a wall to make an embankment. Each of the Springfield forts had at least two bastions, special structures at the corners where artillery was placed.

Fort No. 1, also called Fort Brown, was located about one and a quarter miles northwest of the square on an area of high ground bounded approximately by present-day Kansas Expressway, Nettleton Street, Brower Street, and Chestnut Street. Covering about ten acres, it was by far the largest of the Springfield forts. It was pentagonal in shape, with a bastion at each of the five points.

Fort No. 2 was a small, square-shaped redoubt south of Fort No. 1 at the northeast corner of present-day Walnut and Fort Streets. Both it and Fort No. 1 received their water supply from the nearby Fulbright Spring.

Plans called for Fort No. 3 to be located in the north part of town, slightly west of Boonville, near Josiah Leedy's brickyard. However, work was apparently never commenced on the breastworks there.

Fort No. 4 was located due south of the square on the east side of South Street just north of Mount Vernon Street. It, like Fort No. 2, was small and square shaped, with two bastions placed at opposite corners, and rifle pits connected the two like forts.

Fort No. 5 was located east of the square on the north side of St. Louis Street near present-day John Q. Hammons Parkway. Covering about four acres, it was the second largest of the Springfield forts.

The site of Fort No. 4 on South Avenue at Mount Vernon Street is a church parking lot today. *Photo by author.*

The Springfield defenses were designed by M. LaRue Harrison, a civil engineer who had come to southwest Missouri as a member of the Thirty-sixth Illinois Infantry. Given permission during the summer of 1862 to organize the refugees who had fled to Cassville and Springfield from northern Arkansas into a regiment for the Federal army, he was commissioned a colonel of the First Arkansas Cavalry (Union) and was still recruiting even as construction of the earthworks began.

Near the end of August, Brigadier General James Totten reached Springfield with about 1,200 reinforcements and assumed command of the Southwest District. His first order of business was to make completion of the fortifications a top priority, and he issued a directive that required all prisoners of war, slaves, contrabands (i.e., runaway slaves), soldiers of the garrison, and able-bodied male citizens of Springfield not otherwise employed by the army to work at the forts. To facilitate the order, he further directed that businesses in Springfield could stay open only two hours per day so that the rest of the time could be devoted to working on the emplacements.

An unknown soldier in the Nineteenth Iowa Infantry described the situation at Springfield when he arrived on September 24:

> *Springfield is a pretty town containing some fine buildings and pretty residences.*
>
> *But all business but that of the government is stopped. All business offices, houses, and stores seem to be the places of sutlers or for government business. The character "U.S." stares at you on every sign, upon every horse and mule, and glistens in the sunshine upon every man. One or two eating houses seem to be the only places that wish to do anything, and these are not allowed but a couple of hours a day to remain open.*
>
> *A law compels every man to work a certain portion of his time on the fortifications.*

The soldier's diary entry the next day added, "This portion of Missouri is much the best I have yet seen…I have noticed many fine farms and orchards enclosed by stone fences and on which have been fine residences but which have been burned, the fences broken down, and farms and orchards laid waste."

On the evening of September 28, the soldier and his comrades received orders for their entire company to report to the fortifications the next morning. Benjamin F. McIntyre—who also served in the Nineteenth Iowa and whose diary is so similar to that of the unknown soldier that it suggests that McIntyre might have written both of them—continued the story of what happened the next day: "Our company was formed into a line this morning and marched to the fort in the NW part of the city and informed it would be our duty to guard butternut prisoners. All the other companies of our regiment is at work on the fortifications."

"Butternut" was a disparaging term that Northerners used in reference to Southern soldiers, especially in Missouri, because of the brown, homemade clothes they often wore. For many Northern soldiers, the contemptuous attitude inherent in the term extended to the civilians they encountered in the region as well, even those who professed to be unionists. For instance, William G. Thompson, an officer in another Iowa regiment who arrived in Springfield the same time as McIntyre, told his wife in a letter dated September 25, "The people here prefers to be Union, but their loyalty is only skin deep, and I would not trust many of them further than I could throw a fly."

Ditch digging at the fortifications, of course, was backbreaking work, and slackers often tried to avoid such labor. To induce soldiers to volunteer for the work, or to at least make it more palatable, the army offered an incentive of twenty-five cents per day extra pay for any man who worked on the forts for ten days, due in a lump sum at the end of the ten days. McIntyre, however, considered the offer a sham because he had never met a soldier who had worked at the forts for ten days. Anyone who had worked nine days was always told that his services were not needed on the tenth.

Most of McIntyre's regiment continued to see "shovel and pick duty at the forts" through the first week of October. The Nineteenth Iowa then left Springfield on October 11 to reinforce the Federal troops who had driven the Confederates out of Newtonia.

McIntyre might have been correct that few soldiers worked as many as ten days on the forts. This was not true of slaves and probably was not true of prisoners, but they, unlike the soldiers, were apparently rewarded for their hard labor. For instance, a nineteen-year-old slave named

Robert, belonging to George B. Young, was exempted from working at the fortifications in Springfield during the fall of 1862 because he had already worked twelve days.

Despite the seemingly all-consuming nature of the work on the entrenchments, other activities besides fort building were carried on in Springfield during the fall of 1862. The number of soldiers at Springfield in late September, at least on a temporary basis, approached twenty thousand. Yet no more than about two thousand men, including nonsoldiers, were employed at the fortifications at any given time. Routine camp activities like drill, dress parade, and guard duty occupied much of the soldiers' time, but there were less mundane happenings as well.

A few soldiers, particularly young officers, even found time for romance. Captain William P. Black, who earlier in the summer had a brief dalliance with General Brown's sixteen-year-old daughter, wrote from Springfield in a letter to his mother on September 8, "Since my stay in this place, I have been pleasantly employed in an occasional flirtation with some of these pretty secessionists in this town."

Most of the soldiers, though, even those not at work on the forts, had little time or opportunity for affairs of the heart. A good number spent most of their time guarding prisoners. The college building on the north side of State Street between Campbell and Market had been turned into a prison, and the courthouse was also still being used as a jail. Prisoners, many of them guerrillas captured in the rural areas of southwest Missouri, were brought into town almost on a daily basis. Sergeant McIntyre, speaking of a group of inmates detailed to work on Fort No. 1, claimed that the prisoners were treated as well or better than the soldiers: "Their families are allowed the privilege of visiting them, many remaining for days. They have a good supply of rations, in fact more and of a better quality than we receive."

Other soldiers beat the bushes for guerrillas in the rural areas around Springfield. In the town itself, few Southern-sympathizing citizens remained by the autumn of 1862. The results of the fall election in early November, when a slate of Emancipationist candidates outpolled the Conservative Unionists or Anti-Emancipationists in every instance, show just how far the political winds in Greene County had shifted toward Radical Unionism.

Most fervent Southern sympathizers had fled, while many lukewarm ones who had stayed scarcely balked at taking the oath of allegiance. In late October, for instance, a sixteen-year-old Greene County lad named George Washington Williams was arrested on suspicion of being a Rebel, but he took an oath, swearing that he was "a Union boy and always have been." Williams claimed that he had worked two days on the forts and three weeks driving government teams.

The few unrepentant Southerners who cleaved to their Springfield homes continued, of course, to be subject to imprisonment, exile, or, at best, having their property impressed and their slaves liberated. For example, when a black woman who was the slave of a man then in the Southern army was found on September 6 to be staying at the home of Louisa Campbell, widow of John Polk Campbell, the servant was promptly taken from Mrs. Campbell and pressed into service as a worker at the Springfield military hospital. Then, on October 2, Mrs. Campbell was notified that her house would itself be confiscated for hospital purposes, and she was given only until eight o'clock the following morning to vacate the premises. At the direction of Colonel Holland of the EMM, who was a personal friend of the Campbell family, several soldiers helped Louisa load a few of her belongings into a government wagon and moved her to a relative's home outside Springfield.

Additional space probably was, in fact, needed for hospital use, and the Campbell home was not the only house confiscated for that purpose. In mid- to late autumn, the Springfield infirmaries housed about 1,300 patients, and this number grew even larger after the Battle of Prairie Grove in early December, when many of the wounded were brought to Springfield.

Meanwhile, work on the forts continued apace. When General Curtis learned about October 1 of the plan to fortify Springfield, he disapproved of the idea, questioning the expenditure of manpower necessary to build and hold the fortifications, but by then their construction was well underway. At that time, according to the *Springfield Journal*, about 850 men were working on Fort No. 1, 350 on Fort No. 2, 200 on Fort No. 4, and 400 on Fort No. 5. The citizens of the town were mainly employed at Fort No. 4.

Even the intense pace at which the breastworks were being constructed in early October, however, was apparently not fast enough to suit General Totten. Later in the month, he expanded his previous order that all able-bodied male citizens of Springfield be required to work on the forts to include men living within fifteen miles of the town. Work continued, presumably at an even more rapid pace, throughout the remainder of October and into November. It slowed dramatically later in November when troops were ordered to the Arkansas border in the buildup preceding the Battle of Prairie Grove, and the work may have been suspended altogether as winter came on. Fortunately for Springfield, work on Fort No. 4, at the south edge of town, was nearing completion as 1862 drew to a close.

Chapter 10

Marmaduke's Invasion of Missouri

After the Battle of Prairie Grove in early December 1862, Confederate major general Thomas C. Hindman's First Corps, Trans-Mississippi Army, was forced to retreat to Van Buren, Arkansas. Because of lack of sufficient forage in the vicinity to sustain his whole army, Hindman sent Brigadier General John S. Marmaduke, commanding the Fourth Division of the First Corps, one hundred miles southeast along the Arkansas River to Lewisburg. Later in the month, the Union's Army of the Frontier, following up on its victory at Prairie Grove, began to press the Confederates in the Van Buren area. Hoping to relieve the pressure on his main body and perhaps force a Union withdrawal, Hindman ordered Marmaduke to march north and strike the Federals in the flank or rear.

Marmaduke started north on December 31. His command of about two thousand men consisted of Colonel Joseph O. "Jo" Shelby's Missouri Cavalry Brigade and Colonel Emmett MacDonald's regiment of Missouri cavalry. Another small brigade of about eight hundred men, under command of Colonel Joseph C. Porter, was ordered to cooperate with Marmaduke, and Porter started north from Pocahontas, Arkansas, about the same time. In the colorful words of Major John N. Edwards, Shelby's chief of staff and assistant adjutant general, "On the last day of December, 1862, when the old year was dying in the lap of the new, and January had sent its moaning winds to wail the requiem of the past," the Confederates "were on the march for foray on the border's side."

John S. Marmaduke, who led the Confederate attack on Springfield in January 1863, was elected governor of Missouri after the war. General John S. Marmaduke, #31542, in the collection of Wilson's Creek National Battlefield. *Courtesy of National Park Service.*

The western column under Marmaduke marched north through Arkansas to Yellville, forded the White River at Dubuque on January 6, 1863, and crossed into Missouri to camp on Beaver Creek in Taney County at four o'clock that afternoon. That evening, Marmaduke dispatched Colonel MacDonald on a northeasterly detour to attack Fort Lawrence at Beaver Station in the southwest corner of present-day Douglas County. Still in camp on the same night, Marmaduke learned from scouts and civilian informants that Springfield, although strongly fortified, was weakly garrisoned. Feeling that the town could be captured by a surprise attack, he determined to strike Springfield and sent couriers to Porter with orders that he should march to the support of the main Confederate column as rapidly as possible. MacDonald was also informed of the proposed attack and was directed to support it, but he was allowed to continue his side mission.

Meanwhile, Captain Milton Burch, who had left Ozark on January 5 with a detachment of the Fourteenth Missouri State Militia Cavalry on a scouting expedition to Beaver Station and beyond, captured two Rebel prisoners the next day on Big Creek near the Arkansas border, and they told him that Marmaduke had left Dubuque that morning with a force of almost six thousand men headed to Springfield. Burch immediately dispatched a messenger back to Beaver Station. He and his detachment of one hundred men promptly followed, arriving at Beaver Station on the early morning of January 7. After a brief consultation with Major William Turner, commanding the fort and the local Enrolled Missouri Militia, Burch started back to Ozark and was scarcely out of sight when MacDonald launched an assault on Beaver Station. Cut off from the blockhouse by the Confederates, Burch continued his retreat to Ozark, sending word of the attack ahead of him, as the fort was surrendered into Southern hands and put to the torch. Burch reached Ozark at ten o'clock that night. Pausing barely long enough to gather baggage and supplies, the Federals then resumed their flight to Springfield.

The party that Burch had sent ahead, consisting of some of his own Fourteenth Missouri State Militia and a few men of the Seventy-third Enrolled Missouri Militia, reached Springfield on the late afternoon of January 7 and sounded an alarm. Marmaduke, supposedly with six thousand Confederate troops, had burned the fort and mill at Beaver Station and was marching rapidly toward Springfield!

The only regular army force at Springfield was a detachment of about 375 men of the Eighteenth Iowa Infantry under Lieutenant Colonel Thomas Cook. About 450 men of the Third Missouri State Militia under Colonel Walter King were at Springfield on temporary assignment. In addition, there were more than 1,000 sick and wounded in the Springfield hospitals, while several hundred convalescents recently discharged from the hospitals and other transients were camped north of town awaiting transportation.

Considered by many to be a timid warrior, General Brown, who had reassumed command of the Southwest District when the regular army took to the field before Prairie Grove, balked at offering a defense upon first learning of Marmaduke's approach and thought, instead, that a

Local resident Colonel Henry Sheppard helped persuade General Brown not to abandon Springfield. *From Holcombe's* History of Greene County, Missouri.

withdrawal might be advisable. However, several of his officers, notably Colonels Marcus Boyd and Henry Sheppard, urged that the Federals should not abandon Springfield without a fight. Boyd commanded the Seventy-fourth Regiment of the Enrolled Missouri Militia, and Sheppard had succeeded to colonel of the Seventy-second Regiment after C.B. Holland's recent promotion to brigadier general in charge of all of the EMM in southwest Missouri. Both Boyd and Sheppard had their homes in Springfield (as did Holland) and did not want to abandon the town without resistance.

Although Brown reportedly continued to waffle throughout the night and into the next day, he tentatively agreed to make a stand, and he began organizing the motley group available to him into some semblance of an effective fighting force, as well as making other hasty preparations for defense of the town. He wired dispatches or sent runners to nearby Missouri State Militia posts like Mount Vernon and Cassville urgently requesting reinforcements. Almost 300 men of the Fourth Missouri State Militia under Colonel George H. Hall arrived, and a part of the Fourteenth Missouri State Militia came in under Lieutenant Colonel John Pound. When Captain Burch later arrived from Ozark with his detachment of the Fourteenth, the number of men under Colonel Pound was about 225.

General Holland sent out messengers, calling up the Enrolled Missouri Militia throughout Greene County and beyond. Holland's order to Colonel J.W. Johnson, whose Twenty-sixth EMM was headquartered at Bolivar, read, "You will at once order in your companies and bring them to this post." The other commanders received similar orders. A young woman who was staying in Colonel Sheppard's Springfield home as a houseguest and tutor for his children recalled that the colonel was "up all night sending runners for his men who were enjoying the holidays at their own homes." About two or three hundred EMM, including portions of the Seventy-second and Seventy-fourth Regiments and perhaps a few men of the Twenty-sixth, responded to the call to arms.

Brown authorized Dr. Melcher to organize all of the hospitalized men capable of carrying a gun, who numbered about three hundred, into a company. They were joined by more than one hundred of the transients, and the combined force, later dubbed the "Quinine Brigade," was placed under the overall command of Captain Charles B. McAfee. A number of private citizens also volunteered to aid in defense of their town, and they, along with the Quinine Brigade, were marched to the armory at the Methodist church on the corner of South and Walnut and supplied with what arms happened to be available. All told, Brown had a force of about two thousand men at his disposal.

In addition to gathering and organizing troops, General Brown and his officers were busy during the night of January 7 and into the morning of the eighth making other preparations as well. Fort No. 1, with two brass six-pounders, was the only fort where artillery had already been emplaced. Three old guns, a six-pounder and two twelve-pound howitzers, which were lying virtually abandoned on the grounds of the Calvary Presbyterian Church at Cherry and Jefferson, were hastily rigged up and called into service. Under the supervision of Lieutenant Joseph Hoffman of Backoff's First Missouri Light Artillery, who was recruited from one of the hospitals, the guns were mounted on wagon wheels as temporary carriages, taken to a blacksmith shop for repair, and then rolled to Fort No. 4 and placed in position. Brick buildings were pierced for musketry, while rations and other provisions were moved to the forts or loaded onto wagons and started north toward Bolivar. Contingency plans to destroy the arsenal were made in case it became necessary to abandon Springfield.

News of the Confederate approach threw the citizens of Springfield into a frenzy. The evening of January 7, according to Holcombe, was "a night of excitement, alarm, and terror" for residents of the town. Many hastily packed a few belongings and went to the homes of friends or relatives in the country. Others waited until the next morning, when a battle was imminent, before seeking sanctuary at Fort No. 1 or moving from the exposed fringes of town to the centrally located public square. Some simply hid in their cellars or other places of concealment. For example, music professor John B. Beiderlinden and his family, who lived on South Street just north of Fort No. 4, crawled into the cellar of an outbuilding on their property and stayed there throughout the battle.

The few Southern sympathizers who remained in Springfield, on the other hand, welcomed the prospect of a Confederate invasion and occupation of Springfield. After commenting on the flurry of activity in Springfield on the night of January 7, a correspondent of the *New York Times* whose penname was "Kickapoo" added, "Even some of the secesh women here were busy preparing to feast the rebel officers upon their arrival."

Meanwhile, south of Springfield in Christian County, the Confederates reached Ozark at about ten or eleven o'clock on the evening of January 7, just after Captain Burch had absconded. Shelby sent a detachment around the town to try to cut off Burch's retreat but found that the Federals had already "left in hot haste." Shelby then entered Ozark, cautiously feeling his way through the town until he was entirely satisfied that all the Federals were gone. Finding that "the nest was there and it was warm, but the birds had flown," he set fire to the fort and barracks and destroyed all the food and supplies left by the Federals that his men could not immediately use. By midnight, according to Edwards, the Confederates were again marching north:

> *It was an intensely cold night, that of the 7th, and the frost hung heavy and chill on the garments of my devoted brigade, marching on to the stronghold of the enemy with a determination in their hearts rarely surpassed.*

Joseph O. "Jo" Shelby's brigade constituted the main Confederate force during Marmaduke's invasion of Missouri, including the Battle of Springfield. General Joseph O. Shelby, #31493, in the collection of Wilson's Creek National Battlefield. *Courtesy of National Park Service.*

> *The sun came up on the morning of the 8th like a ball of fire, and the day was gloomy and chill; but Springfield loomed up before us in the distance like a beautiful panorama, and the men, catching the inspiration of the scene, forgot all their trials and hardships, and were eager for the rough, red fray.*

Captain Burch and his detachment came into Springfield at about daybreak on the morning of January 8 and reported that they had been driven out of Ozark and that the Confederates were close on their heels and taking dead aim at Springfield. Fueled now by a sense of urgency, Brown set about hastily disposing his forces and making other last-minute preparations for the looming battle. Lieutenant Hoffman and his makeshift battery occupied Fort No. 4 in the south part of town. They were joined at the fort by a company of the Seventy-fourth EMM under Captain Green B. Phillips and by some of the convalescents and citizens. The cavalry, consisting of detachments of the Third, Fourth, and Fourteenth Missouri State Militia, were positioned to the left or east of Fort No. 4, commanding the southeast part of Springfield. Some of the cavalry was thrown forward as scouting parties to locate the Rebels, and pickets were also posted south of town not far from the Phelps farm. The brick college building west of Fort No. 4 was surrounded on three sides by a palisade, offering a strong defensive position; the prisoners who had been housed there were taken out and moved to the county jail.

Brown ordered that the college be used as a blockhouse, but by some oversight, it was never manned or was insufficiently filled, although some of the Quinine Brigade were stationed near it. A detachment of convalescents and citizens was also posted at the arsenal. Colonel Sheppard's Seventy-second Enrolled Missouri Militia, initially stationed downtown, was brought up to the right or west of the college, while a detachment of the Eighteenth Iowa Infantry was stationed farther west at Fort No. 2. Most of the Eighteenth Iowa, serving as a last defense, occupied Fort No. 1 about half a mile to the rear of the Federal line. The Seventy-fourth EMM, minus Phillips's company, was also garrisoned there, as were some of the citizens.

Marmaduke reached the outskirts of town shortly after sunup on the morning of January 8, but he delayed an attack while reconnoitering the Federal position and waiting for MacDonald's regiment to arrive after its sortie to Beaver Station. The previously indecisive Brown reportedly climbed the courthouse tower, saw through his binoculars that Marmaduke did not have as many men as had been previously reported, and determined for the first time to fight in earnest. Meanwhile, Marmaduke bided his time near the Phelps farm on the edge of town.

Chapter 11

The Battle of Springfield

When MacDonald reached the Confederate camp at about 10:00 a.m., Marmaduke promptly deployed his forces in a battle line running from the St. Louis Road east of town to the Wire Road southwest of town. Shelby's brigade—consisting of Lieutenant Colonel B. Frank Gordon's First Regiment, Lieutenant Colonel Charles A. Gilkey's Second Regiment, Colonel Gideon W. Thompson's Third Regiment, a two-gun battery under Lieutenant Richard A. Collins, a battalion of scouts under Major Ben Elliott, and William Quantrill's partisan company under Lieutenant William Gregg—formed the Confederate right, stretching from the St. Louis Road to the Ozark Road. MacDonald's regiment, with one company dismounted, was positioned to the west of Shelby's brigade, extending all the way to the Wire Road.

Shelby dismounted the First and Third Regiments to fight as infantry but kept Gilkey's regiment in the saddle as the Confederates began their advance to feel out the enemy position. In short order, Gilkey's regiment was also dismounted, leaving just Elliott and Gregg's commands on the far right and most of MacDonald's regiment on the left to fight as cavalry. The Union pickets and scouting parties of cavalry that had been sent forward gradually withdrew toward Fort No. 4 in the face of the methodical Confederate advance, skirmishing as they retreated. It was now apparent that the Confederate attack would come from the south and southeast, and General Brown ordered a number of houses in front

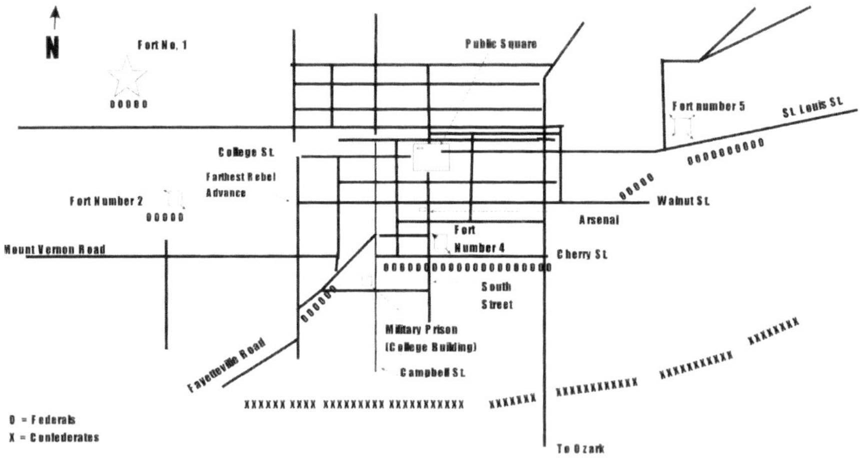

Civil War–era map of Springfield showing the location of fortifications and the initial disposition of forces during the Battle of Springfield.

of Fort No. 4 burned so as to destroy potential hiding places for the enemy and give his gunners a clearer view of the Rebel advance.

Shortly after noon, Colonel King's Third Missouri State Militia was ordered forward to meet the Confederate right and try to stall its advance, but the Federals quickly retreated when Shelby turned his artillery and concentrated his fire on them. Colonel Hall's Fourth Missouri State Militia then took up the charge, advancing against the Rebel center, but Hall also soon withdrew in the face of the superior Confederate fire. A *New York Times* correspondent (the aforementioned "Kickapoo"), who apparently viewed the action from the vantage of Fort No. 4, described the initial skirmishing: "I watched our brave boys gallop forward to the charge, then saw the enemy galloping in a long line to meet them, and heard the sharp, rapid firing of carbines, on both sides. After each charge and fire both parties would turn and gallop back, with small loss on either side." Upon falling back, King's Third MSM took up a defensive position along St. Louis Street, while Hall's MSM retreated through present-day Jenny Lincoln Park and formed a line of defense along Cherry/Mount Vernon Street, in the vicinity of Fort No. 4.

As the Southerners advanced, Collins's battery, stationed in the middle of the Rebel line, paused occasionally to try the range of its rifled artillery piece, and the firing of small arms also increased as the Confederates drew slowly closer. In town, the last of the convalescents and citizens were still being armed and assigned their positions even as the skirmishing on the outskirts was underway in the late morning and early afternoon.

The battle began in earnest at about 1:00 p.m. when Elliott's battalion and Gregg's partisans charged the Union right, probing for a weakness in the Federal defense along St. Louis Street, where Colonel Pound's Fourteenth Missouri State Militia Cavalry and Colonel King's Third MSM were stationed east and west of Benton/Kimbrough Street. Marmaduke thought that an approach to the town along Jordan Creek might be accomplished by such a movement, but Colonel Pound launched a countercharge before the Confederates reached St. Louis and, aided by Colonel King, checked the Rebel assault. After driving Elliott and Gregg back a short distance, King's mounted troops broke off pursuit and returned to St. Louis Street to resume a defensive position.

Meanwhile, the action at and near Fort No. 4 started to intensify as Shelby brought up his two big guns and opened on the fort and town. In the words of Colonel Benjamin Crabb of the Nineteenth Iowa Infantry, who had command of the Springfield post, the Confederates "were busy with their artillery throwing shot and shell at the fort and into the houses occupied by our troops."

Some Springfieldians afterward criticized the Confederates for bombarding the town without issuing a warning to remove the women and children, although Holcombe allowed in his 1883 county history that it was not certain that the Federal battery at Fort No. 4 under Lieutenant Hoffman did not open the artillery duel by shelling Marmaduke's advance. At any rate, Collins unlimbered and, in Holcombe's words, "soon was banging away, his balls falling about the fort and into and near the square in quite rapid succession, and with very uncomfortable precision." One ball struck the Lyon House just off the square on South Street, and two other shots hit the Methodist church at South and Walnut then being used as an arsenal.

The improvised battery at Fort No. 2 promptly replied to the Rebel barrage, with General Brown, who had stationed himself at the southwest bastion, personally directing the firing. "For a time," according to Holcombe, "there was quite a free interchange of metallic compliments between Lieut. Hoffman and Dick Collins." Although Colonel Crabb credited Hoffman and Captain John A. Landis, who had charge of one of the artillery pieces at the fort, with driving the Confederates back, he conceded that the firing from the Union guns was "not sufficiently rapid, owing to their being manned by volunteers, with only five artillery soldiers at the three pieces."

Other observers also blamed the Union's lack of experienced gunners with making the task at hand more daunting than it otherwise might have been. A member of the Third Missouri State Militia remarked shortly after the battle, "The Secesh had two pieces of artillery and they worked them pretty well. We had two pieces of cannon but nobody to work them that knowed anything about it, so you can see the way we stood and you can guess whether we had to fight to keep them out of town or not."

After the attack on Fort No. 4 was repelled, Marmaduke decided that the Confederates were extended too far to the west. He ordered Colonel MacDonald to move his regiment toward the center of the Federal line and to advance on the houses just west of the fort. Re-forming out on the prairie south and slightly west of Fort No. 4 at about 2:00 p. m., MacDonald drew his men up in a line facing the houses and ordered a charge. The Federals stationed in and around the first few houses retreated with little resistance, but when MacDonald's men reached the houses, the Fourth Missouri State Militia mounted a countercharge and drove the Confederates back. Hoping to press the Federal advantage, Captain Landis moved forward his piece of artillery, supported by parts of three companies of the Eighteenth Iowa Infantry, to the front and right of the fort, in the vicinity of State Street just east of Campbell.

Seeing that MacDonald was sorely pressed, Shelby promptly ordered Colonel Gordon and Colonel Gilkey to "charge with their regiments to support MacDonald." In response, according to Edwards, "a thousand warriors sprang to their feet, and, with one wild Missouri yell, burst upon the foe."

When Shelby's men stormed to MacDonald's rescue, most of the Federals scattered, leaving Landis exposed and too far advanced to safely retreat. A detachment from Gordon and Gilkey's regiments rushed the artillery piece and captured it after a sharp fight in which several of the Iowa infantrymen, including Captains W.R. Blue and

J. Van Meter, were killed or mortally wounded and Captain Landis was severely wounded. David V. Whitney, a surgeon with the Fourth Missouri Militia Cavalry whom Colonel Crabb lauded for fighting alongside his comrades during the battle, dropped his weapon and hurried to the aid of Captains Blue and Van Meter, but he quickly turned to other wounded men when he realized that the men were beyond help. Meanwhile, the dispersed Federals began retreating to the fort, the rifle pits west of the fort, and other shelters at the edge of town.

Surgeon David V. Whitney of the Fourth Missouri State Militia Cavalry took an active part in defending the town during the Battle of Springfield. Surgeon David V. Whitney, #11497, in the collection of Wilson's Creek National Battlefield. *Courtesy of National Park Service.*

With the Federals having been driven back, the Confederates now advanced into the edge of town, moving "from house to house and from fence to fence," according to Major G.W.C. Bennett of MacDonald's regiment. The Rebels took possession of the college building that had previously been used as a prison and occupied it as a stronghold for the rest of the day, and they also gained control of a number of houses in the surrounding neighborhood, called Dutch Town.

Shelby now ordered forward the Third Regiment under Colonel Thompson and the two guns of Collins's battery, one of which was "brought up into the very town," where it opened "at point-blank range."

The Quinine Brigade, most of which had heretofore been stationed in and around brick buildings near the center of Springfield, was advanced to the line of battle to reinforce the Missouri State Militia cavalry and the detachments of Iowa infantry already there. Colonel Crabb, assisted by Lieutenants R. Root of the Nineteenth Iowa Infantry, S.A. Wilson of the Eighteenth Iowa, and William F. Bodenhammer of the Twenty-fourth Missouri Infantry, took charge of the convalescents and posted them in front of and to the west of Fort No. 4 behind a fence, about fifty to seventy-five yards from the Rebels, who were also positioned behind fences and in and around a house to the Federal front. The two sides fired away at each other from close range.

In Edwards's words, "The Federals, re-enforced largely…came back with cavalry and artillery, and a hot, desperate conflict ensued; one side struggling to hold the position gained, the other to drive them from it. Bravely my fighting brigade meets the onset, and stubbornly they resist; blow falls on blow, shot follows shot…The contest rages, and the wild death-dance goes merrily on."

Colonel Crabb apparently took a less quixotic view of the scene than did Major Edwards. Describing the action from the Federal standpoint in more matter-of-fact terms, Crabb merely said, "After fighting for nearly an hour, the enemy gave way and fled precipitately from the field."

Whether the Confederates "fled precipitately" is likely a matter of perspective, but the fighting near Fort No. 4 slackened at midafternoon, as the Confederates in that vicinity drew back and began instead pressing the Union right, which was defended mainly by Colonel Sheppard's regiment of Enrolled Missouri Militia stationed in the southwest part of town along or just north of State Street. In response to the Rebel movements, much of the Missouri State Militia Cavalry was repositioned to the west, the Third MSM shifting to the right of Sheppard's men and the Fourth MSM still farther west. As Holcombe noted, there was a lot of "galloping about on the part of the officers" during the battle and "a great deal of 'double-quicking' on the part of the men as they hurried from one part of town to the other."

As the fighting shifted westward, General Brown rode forward along South Street with his body guard to near the corner of State to oversee the battle and encourage his men. While there, consulting with some of his officers, he was shot from his horse by a Rebel sharpshooter concealed in a house or other nearby hiding place. Brown was taken to the rear with a severely wounded arm, the bone having been broken above the left elbow, and he officially turned over command of the Union troops engaged in the battle to Colonel Crabb. Later, a piece of the bone was removed from Brown's arm during a successful operation that saved it from amputation.

Shelby dismounted the men of Elliott's battalion and brought them up to support Collins's iron six-pound artillery piece for his assault on the Union right, where, in the words of General Holland, "the hardest and most decisive fighting of the day took place." As the Confederates doggedly advanced, the six-pounder was moved to a position just west of Market Street, and the artillerists opened on the Federals to their front, throwing grape and canister into their midst. Meanwhile, the Rebels had also "gained possession of several houses," according to Colonel Crabb, "and were pouring into our ranks volley after volley of musketry," and "the cause became desperate."

General Colley B. Holland commanded the Enrolled Missouri Militia during the Battle of Springfield. *Courtesy of History Museum for Springfield–Greene County.*

Said Kickapoo, "The enemy now approached in good order, until they came within gunshot, when they began to crawl upon the ground, like Indians, with admirable skill, from one stump to another, sheltering themselves as much as possible, but keeping up a deadly fire…The crack of rifles was continuous, like the roll of thunder, and the enemy's grape hurtled along over our heads in a way that was dangerous."

At first, the Seventy-second Enrolled Missouri Militia—supported by detachments of the Quinine Brigade, the Missouri State Militia Cavalry, and the Eighteenth Iowa Infantry—stubbornly resisted the Confederate onslaught. Some of the fiercest fighting of the engagement took place in and around the city cemetery, located just east of the college building in the northeast quadrant of Campbell and State. "Back and forth through the aisles and across the graves of the silent sleepers," said Holcombe, "ran blue coats and gray jackets, and through the trees, where nothing but birds had sung and soft breezes had blown aforetime, now whistled the cannon shot and shrieked the bombshell."

Most of the Confederates were now out of range of the small arms fire from Fort No. 4, but the Federal artillery stationed there continued, in the words of Colonel Crabb, "to pour a heavy fire of shot and shell into their midst, which would cause them to falter, but they would again and again rally. The stockade fort, which they had previously taken possession of, gave them great protection, and in and around which they would mass their forces, and from which they would make their charges. They would drive our men, and then in turn be driven back."

Major Bennett of MacDonald's regiment also remarked on the back-and-forth nature of the action: "We advanced twice, occupying the houses in front of the fort; but the enemy being largely re-enforced, we found we could not hold them without an unnecessary loss of life, and we returned inside the palisades."

A correspondent of the *St. Louis Daily Missouri Republican* described the action in similar terms:

> *The fight now became general…The principal fighting…was west of the Fort, near the college formerly used as a prison. This college is of brick, and is surrounded by a stockade. The rebels obtained possession of it, and found it almost as safe as a regular fort. They also stationed*

> *themselves in houses. Our men were in and behind other houses. Some of them lay behind fences. The firing was constant. All organization seemed to be at an end. It was every man for himself, and God for us all; but instead of running for themselves, the men fought bravely.*

After an hour of hard fighting, however, the Federals started giving ground. In Crabb's words, "The enemy were pressing hard upon our brave men, and they were yielding before the overwhelming numbers brought against them…It was one continual roar of musketry and artillery."

According to General Holland, Colonel Sheppard and his EMM were "compelled to fall back in the direction of Fort No. 1, taking advantage of the scattered houses to continue the fight as they retired."

At about four o'clock, a messenger came to Colonel Sheppard's house and reported that General Brown had been wounded and that the Rebels had driven the Federals back and were fighting desperately. The "Yankee girl" who was staying at the Sheppard home as a tutor recalled:

> *I knew from their unearthly yells they were gaining upon us. There were about 30 women and children in the house besides Colonel S.'s family; some were wringing their hands and crying, "Oh God, spare my husband!"…I was thankful I had no husband to be used as a target on that day. Whichever way I turned, faces were looking at me, filled with despair; and groans from anxious hearts only replied to my words of comfort.*

Although General Holland claimed that Sheppard's men retreated grudgingly and kept up a fight even as they dropped back, other observers have been less charitable to the militiamen in their assessment of the action. Holcombe, for instance, remarked that Sheppard's men "trotted back" in "considerable disorder," despite the efforts of their officers to rally them. Shelby's men followed in close pursuit, and Major A.C. Graves, editor of the *Springfield Journal* and an officer on Colonel Sheppard's staff, was mortally wounded while trying to collect the rattled troops.

The men of the EMM finally halted their flight and re-formed under cover of a hill along College Street, although one squad reportedly raced all the way to Fort No. 1. Reinforced by soldiers from the Eighteenth Iowa

Infantry stationed at Fort No. 2 and by several cavalry companies who had "double-quicked" from the uninvolved east flank, Colonel Sheppard rallied his men and ordered them forward again. They charged up the hill with a shout, and Shelby's men, some of whom had advanced as far as West Walnut Street, were driven back to near State Street, where they once again took shelter in the college building and in and behind houses, "enabling their sharpshooters," according to General Holland, "to check our farther advance."

At about 5:00 p.m., Shelby launched one last assault on the Federal right center near Fort No. 4, making what Colonel Crabb called "the most desperate effort that they had made during the day to drive back our forces." Gilkey's regiment and Elliott's battalion, under the cover of houses and fences, advanced to within about one hundred yards of the fort and opened fire, but they were met by return fire from the Quinine Brigade, Captain Phillips's company of the Seventy-fourth EMM, the Fourth Missouri State Militia Cavalry (dismounted), the Second Battalion of the Fourteenth Missouri State Militia Cavalry (dismounted), parts of five companies of the Eighteenth Iowa Infantry, and some of Sheppard's Seventy-second EMM, totaling about eight hundred men. After a sharp exchange that lasted almost half an hour, part of the Federal line began to waver, and an officer in the Second Battalion of the Fourteenth MSM ordered his troops to their horses. The entire battalion went charging to the rear and took to their mounts, as Colonel Crabb tried in vain to rally the terrified soldiers. The panic among the Fourteenth MSM caused the rest of the command to balk momentarily as well, but Crabb was able to rally the remaining troops, who promptly "went again into the fight."

Lieutenant Colonel Pound, too, was soon able to collect his frightened troops, and the Fourteenth also once again advanced. The Confederates fired just a few more rounds before giving up their attempt to storm the fort as a bad job and retiring from the field as darkness came on. Five more companies of the Eighteenth Iowa Infantry, previously stationed at Fort No. 1, then "came to the rescue," according to Colonel Crabb, "whooping and cheering." They arrived too late to take an active part in the engagement but gave fresh courage to the troops already involved, as the latter group drove the Rebels back into the shelter of the college stockade.

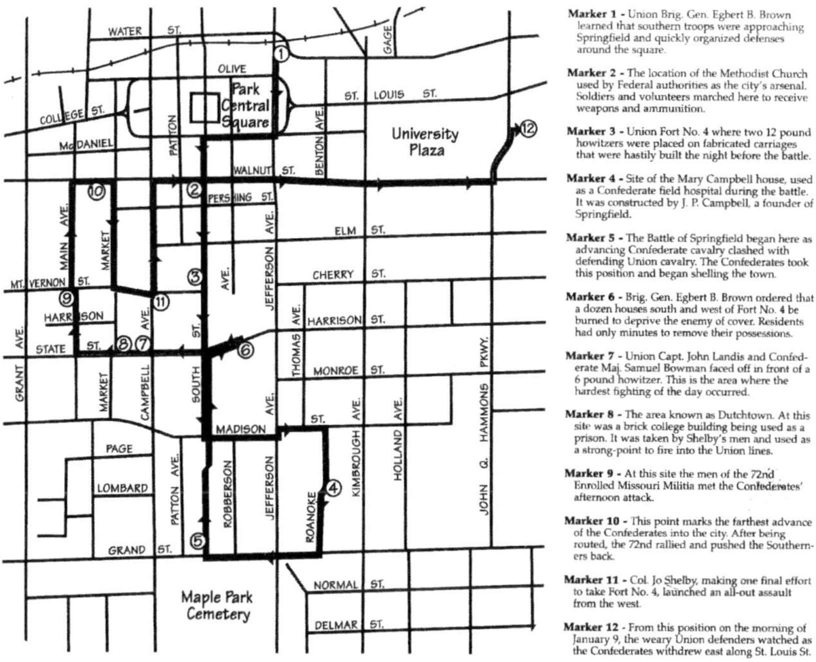

Battle of Springfield map showing historical marker tour route. *Map produced by Wilson's Creek National Battlefield Foundation.*

"Darkness coming on," said Colonel Crabb, "the firing gradually ceased." General Holland and General Marmaduke, too, noted the role that the approach of nighttime played in ending the battle, but only Major Edwards was inspired to poetic heights by the dimming day: "Night came down with weary, brooding wings, laid her dark brow across the cloudy sky, and threw her sable mantle over fort and wall and house and men, checking the bloody strife, and calming the furious passions that had been at war all day."

Only sporadic firing of artillery broke the evening stillness during the next few hours, as the Confederates continued to occupy the college building and the stockade surrounding it. According to Edwards, Collins "made a promenade upon the principal streets of the city" with his iron six-pounder, firing at whatever target happened to present itself, and the artillery at Fort No. 4 occasionally answered.

Late that night, the Rebels abandoned the college building and drew off to the Phelps farm. "The men here bivouacked for the night," according to Major Bennett, "and, building large fires from the fine oak fence rails of mine host Phelps, and with a plentiful supply from the richly stored larder of Mrs. Phelps, regaled themselves after the hard day's fight."

Remaining on alert throughout the night, the Federals expected Marmaduke to resume the battle the next morning, but instead he moved off to the east, having "deemed it best not to renew the attack," because Union reinforcements in the form of additional Enrolled Missouri Militia from the surrounding area had reached Springfield in the early morning, and he felt that his weary troops were in no condition for another desperate fight. Not surprisingly, Major Edwards, in his customarily florid style, offered a more romantic rationale for the Confederate withdrawal: "The mission had been accomplished; two forts had been captured, a piece of artillery taken, several hundred prisoners paroled, considerable commissary stores destroyed, and we, after making almost a circuit of the town with floating banners and waving pennons, left it alone in its glory, because all had been done that could be done."

A reconnaissance party of Federal cavalry rode out toward the Confederates as they circled the town to the east, but the Rebels declined the invitation and continued their march toward Hartville, where Marmaduke and Porter finally met up and were defeated by Federal forces in a battle on January 11.

In the days following the Battle of Springfield, a few reports arose that the Enrolled Missouri Militia had behaved in a less than gallant manner during the fighting, but a number of observers sprang to the defense of the local militia. Rejoicing over the outcome of the battle, the young woman who was staying at the Sheppard home, for example, claimed that "Col. Sheppard and Gen. Holland covered themselves with glory."

Like the loyal citizens of Springfield and the surrounding region, Federal authorities also cheered the news of the Union victory. For instance, General Curtis, commanding the Department of the Missouri, sent a dispatch to General Brown congratulating him on his "gallant and successful defense of Springfield…The troops and people of Springfield who participated in your efforts have given imperishable proof of their loyal devotion to our cause and country, and the State of Missouri will cherish your memory."

On the other hand, the secessionists who remained in Springfield were, of course, disappointed in the outcome of the battle. In the words of Kickapoo, they had been "delighted in the morning" but were "at night, crestfallen."

The homes of several Union families had been burned, and many others had been pierced by shot and shell. Windows throughout the town had been shattered and fences knocked down. "Ruin and desolation were everywhere," continued Kickapoo, "but our victory compensates for all."

Casualties at the Battle of Springfield were about equal for both sides. Federal officers reported 14 killed, 146 wounded, and 5 missing or captured, for a total of 165 casualties. Marmaduke reported 19 killed, 105 wounded, and 26 missing, for a total loss of 150.

However, the outcome was a significant Federal victory because it saved the town of Springfield and preserved its vast store of supplies for the Army of the Frontier. The only consolation that the Confederates could take from the engagement was that it did partially achieve General Hindman's objective of relieving the pressure on his embattled troops in Arkansas by inducing a large withdrawal of Federal soldiers from that state to protect southwest Missouri. Springfield, however, would never again be seriously threatened by Southern forces, and the town, in stark contrast to its fate during the first half of the war, would even prosper to some extent during the second half.

Chapter 12

The Second Half of the War

After the battle of January 8, 1863, Springfield would not witness another significant military action in its vicinity, and the town quickly settled into a period of relative calm under Union rule that would last throughout the remainder of the war. No longer distraught by the immediate threat of war, the townspeople began trying to restore a semblance of normalcy, and their attention gradually turned to the mundane tasks of ordinary life. Businesses thrived, and the civil courts, although still supplemented by martial law, were kept busy. Despite the buzz of activity, poverty continued to plague the town, as destitute refugees swarmed the streets overwhelming the relief efforts of religious and charitable organizations.

Military and civilian authorities alike usually worried as much about vice and other crime as they did about any threat posed by the enemy. Outside town, the marauding gangs of bushwhackers that still infested the countryside presented the biggest military threat, and ferreting them out was the greatest challenge faced by many Union soldiers stationed at Springfield. In short, the second half of the Civil War in Springfield was marked not by historic battles but rather by military routine, humanitarian concerns, and everyday civilian life, punctuated by enough notable incidents that they could scarcely be called isolated.

One of the first tasks facing the town after the Battle of Springfield was burial of those who had been killed during the fight. The ceremony took place on Sunday, January 11, at 2:00 p.m. and included a long procession of citizens and soldiers escorting the bodies and the horses of the dead from the public square to the burial ground at the north edge of town near present-day Grant Avenue and Central Street. Near the same time as the Union ceremony, the Confederate dead were buried at the southwest corner of Jefferson and Harrison Streets.

Reinforcements in the form of Colonel William F. Cloud's brigade reached Springfield on January 13, and Cloud succeeded General Brown as commander of the Southwest District less than a month later. About the same time, Colonel Crabb was also relieved of duty as commander of the Springfield post, and he was replaced by Colonel Thomas M. Bowen, who himself was quickly replaced by Colonel John Edwards. Post returns show 1,996 men at Springfield under Edwards at the end of April 1863. Both the district and the post continued to see a succession of commanders throughout the remainder of the war, and the number of soldiers stationed at the post, not counting local militia, continued to average slightly fewer than 2,000 most of the time, although many more might have passed through or been there on temporary assignment at any given time.

One of the more bizarre and sensational incidents of the Civil War in Springfield occurred in early February 1863, less than a month after the Battle of Springfield, when a reward was offered on the head of notorious bushwhacker Alf Bolin, who had long terrorized the people of Taney and surrounding counties. Bolin was killed about the first day of February by a Union soldier posing as a Confederate, and the infamous guerrilla's body was brought into Forsyth on the second. The next day, a detail of soldiers started with the body toward Springfield to collect the reward, but the procession was stopped a mile or so north of Forsyth and the body dissevered from its head by an axe-wielding man whose family had suffered at the hands of the notorious Bolin. The body was subsequently buried, but the soldiers placed the head in a pine box and, resuming their journey, took it with them as evidence of Bolin's death. The head was displayed in Ozark and viewed by many people before the detail continued its trek to Springfield. The box and its gruesome contents reached Springfield on the evening of February 4, when the head was reportedly placed briefly on a pole for public viewing before being turned over to the provost marshal of the post.

Although many of the permanent residents of Springfield saw the quality of their lives vastly improve once the immediate threat of war was reduced, destitute refugees continued to flood the streets, covering the city with a pall of misery. A Springfield correspondent to the *St. Louis Tri-Weekly Missouri Republican* described the desperate situation facing the exiles in early February 1863:

> *The desolations of this historic town are, just now, completely hidden from view by a mantle of the softest, purest snow which ever fell from heaven upon a field of blood. The feathery element lies a foot deep, at least, but no jingle of merry sleigh bells resounds through our streets, for such a snow-storm is almost as unprecedented as the Springfield battle, and there is neither sleigh nor sled in the place. But if snow adds nothing to the gayety of the rich, it certainly adds much to the sufferings of the shoeless children of the poor, of whom Springfield has many.*
>
> *The poor of the city, however, are not native to it. They are refugees from the South, who have fled hither for protection, for shelter, for food and clothing; and here, far from home, scores of them have died and been buried. Some of them are in open houses without a stove or a fire-place; some have not a bed to lie upon; some have not a change of clothing; many of them can find no work, or if they could find it, they are sick and unable to labor. The care of these suffering ones is committed to the Post Chaplain, who has a storehouse of provisions, from which, without a penny of expense to the government, they are weekly fed. The ladies of Springfield meet weekly to sew for them; but in spite of all attention which they may receive, Death claims many of them as his own, and releases them from earthly misery. The Western Sanitary Commission has furnished bedding and hospital clothing for a free hospital, which is to be established for their benefit, and when this is opened a few may be saved from the lonely, horrible death of a pauper.*

The correspondent went on to explain that food for the poor had been provided in three different ways. Part of the funds was raised by charging rent to the tenants of houses owned by absent disloyalists. Part of the money was given to the post chaplain, Reverend Wines, by the War Relief Fund Committee of St. Louis, and part of it was donated by private individuals.

The refugees, however, were still in dire need of clothing, particularly shoes for women and children. The correspondent then informed his readers that donations could be sent to Springfield to the attention of "Rev. Fred H. Wines, Chaplain" and marked "For the Poor."

The Springfield hospitals, according to the correspondent, were not as full as they had been two or three months earlier, but there were still five or six hundred sick and wounded soldiers. Four buildings—the Bailey House Hotel, the Berry house, the courthouse, and the tobacco warehouse—were still being used as hospitals. Most of the wounded Federal soldiers were lodged at the tobacco warehouse, which was a branch of the courthouse hospital.

Like the refugees, at least some of the permanent residents of Greene County, particularly those in the rural areas, also suffered privations. Because of the scarcity and the high price of provisions, some citizens contemplated moving away, and perhaps a few did. Not all local citizens, however, thought that the situation was as dire as the widespread reports of starvation in southwest Missouri might have indicated. In late April 1863, for instance, the editor of the *Springfield Journal*, J.W.D.L.F. Mack, argued that the claims of hardship were exaggerated. "That there has been many cases of want and destitution is certainly true," allowed Editor Mack, or "Alphabet" Mack as he was sometimes called, "but we are prone to make as much fuss and complaint as possible about our misfortunes, and hence we have magnified the bad condition of things here to some extent." Citing the moderate cost of provisions (such as ten cents a dozen for eggs) and a relatively good pay scale for labor (at one to two dollars a day), Mack concluded that the people of Springfield did not suffer "to any considerable extent."

Refugees continued to seek asylum in Springfield throughout the remainder of the war, but their numbers and the extent of their hardship abated somewhat later in the war. In January 1864, for example, a Springfield correspondent to the *St. Louis Missouri Democrat* found it hardly remarkable that the town was home to three hundred destitute refugees who were being fed by the government.

Reverend Frederick H. Wines, mentioned in the *Tri-Weekly Republican* correspondent's report, was personally selected by President Lincoln to be the Union army's post chaplain at Springfield. A graduate of Princeton Seminary, Wines held religious services at the Calvary Presbyterian

Reverend Frederick Wines ministered to Springfieldians from 1862 to 1864. *Courtesy of History Museum for Springfield–Greene County.*

Church, located on South Jefferson Street. According to church history, it was also through Lincoln's direct intervention that Calvary Presbyterian was able to continue services throughout most of the Civil War, despite the conditions of martial law that halted activity at all the other churches in Springfield. Reverend Wines served in Springfield from 1862 through 1864 and was, as the newspaper correspondent's report suggested, instrumental in the relief effort to the town's poor.

In February and March 1863, organization of a new militia force, called the Provisional Enrolled Missouri Militia (PEMM), was conducted throughout the state. The new force was not designed to replace or interfere with the original EMM but instead was to be a permanent force detailed from the original militia for active duty and consisting primarily of men whose everyday jobs were not considered indispensable. The arrangement allowed members of the original EMM to stay home and tend to their crops or perform other necessary civilian duties and only be called up in case of emergency. Most of the officers and many of the men of the Sixth Regiment of the PEMM were drawn from the two Greene County regiments of the original EMM. For instance, Henry Sheppard, formerly colonel of the Seventy-second EMM, was commissioned colonel of the Sixth Regiment of the new provisional militia.

The primary job of the Provisional Enrolled Missouri Militia was hunting the Confederate guerrillas who continued to infest the countryside throughout much of Missouri, including the southwest part. Greene County did not witness the level of atrocity from the marauding Southern bands as did certain other counties in the state, such as those along the Missouri River, where notorious guerrillas like Bill Anderson operated, but the citizens of the county did suffer their share of plundering, robbery, horse theft, and even occasional violence at the hands of bushwhackers. In fact, one of the isolated incidents of violence was authored by Bill Anderson himself when he kidnapped a man named Joseph Cooper in the northwest corner of Greene County and killed him just across the line in Polk County, while the ferocious Bloody Bill and his band were on the way from their winter quarters in Texas to northern Missouri in the spring of 1864.

Not all plundering and violence, however, was instigated by Confederate partisans. A secret and fanatical political organization called the Union League that was similar to its like-named predecessor of the prewar years flourished briefly in Greene County during the Civil War, and its members sometimes perpetuated crimes or avenged private grievances in the name of loyalty. Federal soldiers, too, were sometimes guilty of indiscriminate foraging and other excesses. In January 1864, for example, Brigadier General John B. Sanborn, commanding the District of Southwest Missouri, received numerous complaints at his Springfield headquarters of Federal troops taking so much forage that the farmers were unable to feed their stock. In addition, according to Holcombe, bands of men in Federal service "rode about through the country, and pouncing unawares upon some harmless Confederate

General John B. Sanborn commanded the Southwest District of Missouri, with headquarters at Springfield during the latter half of the war. *From Holcombe's* History of Greene County, Missouri.

sympathizer, plundered him without remorse and sometimes shot him without mercy."

While it is true that Southern sympathizers of Greene County suffered at the hands of unprincipled Federal soldiers just as Union citizens were often the victim of Confederate guerrillas, relatively few cases of foul murder were perpetuated by either side in Greene County, and the few violent crimes that did occur more likely sprang from a base motive like greed than from political considerations. Even Holcombe allowed, for instance, that James M. Thompson, a well-to-do cattle dealer who was ambushed by a murderous gang just south of Springfield in the fall of 1864, was almost certainly killed for his money.

For many Union citizens of Springfield, part of trying to restore a sense of normal life during the second half of the Civil War meant doing what litigious Americans had been prone to do since colonial times: filing lawsuits against their neighbors—particularly, in the case of the Springfield plaintiffs, against absent disloyalists. More than three hundred such suits were filed in Greene County Circuit Court between May 1862 and October 1864. Traditional wisdom, espoused by Holcombe and others, has held that the motivation behind most of the suits was an attempt to gain compensation for property taken or destroyed during the Southern occupation of Springfield. Janice Durbin-Dodd, however, in her 1995 study of the effects of the Civil War on civilians in southwest Missouri, analyzed the court records and concluded that the vast majority of the suits were filed in an effort to gain payment of a debt, not to reclaim property taken or destroyed by the Southerners. The plaintiffs were motivated not so much by a sense of justice but by something less noble. They were, as Ms. Durbin-Dodd has pointed out, "not seeking redress of grievances suffered at the hands of the rebels" but instead merely "wanted to have their bills paid."

For example, in November 1863, Naomi J. McFall filed a suit against Dick Campbell claiming that she had sold him a horse for which he had agreed to pay her $175 but that, when he took possession of the animal, he left Confederate scrip as payment. The money, of course, was worthless in Missouri, and as was almost always the case in suits brought by unionists against absent disloyalists, the Greene County court found in favor of the plaintiff, decreeing that Campbell owed $200 as payment of the debt and court costs. The court further ordered that the defendant's property be attached to cover the $200 and that he be required to appear at the next term of court. Neither Campbell nor any of his property, however, could be found in Greene County.

Some Springfield citizens sought redress of their grievances through military channels rather than the civil courts. For example, Mrs. Permilla Stephens, whose husband, John A. Stephens, had been inadvertently killed by one of Zagonyi's men in the fall of 1861, had suffered a second devastating setback when the rental houses she owned, which provided her sole income after her husband's death, were among those ordered destroyed by General Brown during the preliminary maneuvering at the Battle of Springfield. She petitioned the government for compensation for her loss, but when she had yet to collect anything by November 1863 to satisfy her claim for damages, she applied to Reverend Wines, chaplain in charge of refugees, for rations for her and her children. The minister, in turn, wrote a letter to General Sanborn, commanding the District of Southwest Missouri, arguing that while Mrs. Stephens's case did not strictly come under the guidelines of an order issued by General Schofield, commanding the Department of the Missouri, which authorized free rations to the destitute, the exceptional circumstances of her case warranted special consideration. "I respectfully recommend," concluded Reverend Wines, "that the issue of rations be allowed her as a special favor. I refer the case to you for your decision." The request was promptly approved. (After the war, Mrs. Stephens became the first woman to hold the office of Springfield postmistress.)

Not surprisingly, Southerners who petitioned the government for relief or redress of grievances did not receive as sympathetic a hearing as did Union citizens like Mrs. Stephens. For instance, after Louisa Campbell's home and premises were confiscated by the Union for government purposes, she applied to the military district headquarters in the summer of 1864 for compensation, but the request was denied, partly on the grounds that a portion of the premises was "owned in fee by her sons who are in Arms against the United States."

On July 18, 1864, about the same time that Mrs. Campbell's request for compensation was denied, S.H. "Pony" Boyd, adding insult to injury, wrote a letter to the provost marshal of the Department of the Missouri informing him that Mrs. Campbell had left Springfield on her way to St. Louis and that "we have good reason to believe she has letters to carry to the South." Although the letters probably contained no military secrets but instead were of a personal or family nature, it hardly mattered. The sides had been drawn three years earlier, and the Campbells and the Boyds, both prominent Springfield families, had taken opposite parts. One of the tragic consequences of the Civil War was that it often made enemies of people who had previously been friends.

Several Union military units were organized at Springfield during 1863 and 1864. Among these were the Second Arkansas Cavalry regiment and three batteries of the Second Missouri Artillery. Colonel of the former unit was John E. Phelps, son of John S. Phelps, and the regiment received a big sendoff from the people of Springfield when it left for the war front in the spring of 1864. In addition, the Sixth Provisional Enrolled Missouri Militia was reorganized as the Sixteenth Missouri Cavalry in the summer of 1864.

Even after Lincoln's Emancipation Proclamation in January 1863, which freed the slaves in the seceding states, the question persisted of what to do about blacks in slaveholding but loyal states like Missouri. In Springfield and the surrounding area, blacks who "absquatulated [fled] from their masters and their homes and started on their way to Kansas rejoicing," as the *Springfield Journal* phrased it, remained a particular issue. Calling Kansas "that Paradise of the Contrabands," the editor opined that it was to be regretted when, as sometimes happened, runaway slaves were aided in their flight by abolitionists acting without proper authority, because such interference would only cause ill will.

By 1864, however, the question of what to do about blacks in Missouri had been answered in practice, if not in theory, as they were being actively recruited for Federal service. In January of that year, a correspondent to a St. Louis newspaper reported that the enlistment of blacks at Springfield was progressing favorably under the direction of the provost marshal, Major Oliver P. Newberry, who was "exercising himself to bring into the service every able-bodied negro in this district." Missouri, however, remained an inhospitable place for blacks, and many continued to flee for Kansas or other free states. By January 1865, when an emancipation ordinance was passed in Missouri, only 584 blacks remained in Greene County, whereas the slave population in 1860 had totaled 1,677.

During General Price's invasion of Missouri in the fall of 1864, General Sanborn left Springfield with most of his available troops, including Colonel Phelps's Second Arkansas, to operate against the Confederates. With Springfield left weakly garrisoned, the people were apprehensive for fear that Price might try to attack and capture the town, and occasional rumors circulated that he was actually marching on the town. Sentinels kept a close lookout on all the roads leading into town, but their vigilance proved unnecessary, as the Southerners were soon chased back into Arkansas without ever having approached Springfield.

The fall election of 1864 demonstrated just how much political sentiment had changed in Springfield and Greene County since 1860. For president, Lincoln received more than 2,200 votes in the county, while General George McClellan, his Democrat opponent, received fewer than 350. Radical Republicanism, which had been anathema to most Greene County citizens at the beginning of the war, was now dominant.

Even in the best of times throughout history, corruption in the form of gambling, excessive drinking, and prostitution have tended to thrive anywhere young single men have congregated in large numbers. Springfield during the Civil War was no exception, and the abject poverty of the refugees who took semipermanent haven in the town during the second half of the war merely increased the vice, particularly prostitution. "Hundreds of female refugees swarmed about Springfield and other posts of importance," wrote Holcombe, "and became abandoned and depraved. Vice and immorality of all sorts prevailed."

In late 1862, a Granby woman named Mrs. Reid took refuge in Springfield and was given lodging in a house owned by J.P. Perkins. In December, Perkins applied to the provost marshal's office for her removal, complaining that, although Mrs. Reid herself had always behaved modestly, she had allowed some girls to stay with her who "behaved in a manner unbecoming ladies."

In May 1864, two men who lived near the college prison in south Springfield complained to the assistant provost marshal of two "disorderly women," named Mrs. Rogers and Mrs. Whitstine, who lived in the same vicinity. The men claimed that Mrs. Whitstine had "abused respectable women living in that neighborhood by shameful and indecent talk," that frequent quarrels between soldiers involving firearms took place at the women's house and that both women were "public prostitutes." Summoned to testify in the case, J.W. McClellan swore that, during the previous February while he was employed as a United States detective, he had visited the women's home on several occasions and that he always found officers or soldiers there. "I think they were there for the purpose of having sexual intercourse with her [Mrs. Rogers]," McClellan opined. "I know that different men have been caught in bed with her, and to the best of my knowledge and belief, she is a base prostitute." After the lieutenant commanding the prison also swore out an affidavit recommending the removal of Mrs. Rogers and the "whole she-bang," the two women were declared to be public nuisances and were banished from the District of Southwest Missouri.

Apparently, prostitution was a serious enough problem that it disrupted military discipline. In mid-November 1864, for example, a provost marshal's report from Springfield noted that "[v]enereal disease prevails largely at this post and seriously affects the efficiency of our troops."

Complaints about debauched women continued to filter into the provost marshal's office during the following year. In April 1865, a woman named Mrs. Watkins gave a statement charging five women, whom she considered to be public prostitutes, with "encouraging soldiers into evil ways." The next month, a man living a few miles north of Springfield near a spot where some soldiers were camped complained that four women, who were also camped nearby in a cave, "frequently become intoxicated and by their bad conduct attract the attention of the soldiers, who visit them very frequently."

Perhaps female refugees were sometimes erroneously assumed to be fallen women when they were, instead, respectable people who simply found themselves in dire straits. This was apparently true in the case of Mary Willis, cited in a previous chapter. Miss Willis was shot and killed in the spring of 1862 when two drunken soldiers called at the Willis home, a house previously occupied by accommodating girls. A similar mistaken assumption may also have come into play in the case of Thomas Andrews, a twenty-two-year-old Springfieldian who was arrested for disorderly conduct in January 1864 because of an incident at the Louisa Campbell home, which had been confiscated by the government and was being used as a residence by several female refugees.

In late December 1863, Andrews called at the Campbell house and, when Agnes Crawford answered the door, asked to see Mrs. Crawford's daughter, Mollie. Mrs. Crawford turned the unwanted suitor away, but late the next night, he came back in a drunken state and awakened both Agnes and her daughter by calling for Mollie in a loud voice. When Andrews did not wait to be invited in but instead kicked the door open and started toward Mollie's bed, Mrs. Crawford jumped out of bed and lit a lantern. Mollie, who apparently was acquainted with Andrews, shouted that she wanted something to kill him with, and she and her mother grabbed a poker and a shovel and forced him out of the room. Andrews, however, kicked the door open again and, according to Agnes Crawford, "swore he would cut our God damned hearts out." The mother and daughter were able to get the door closed a second time before Andrews broke it open again and, turning to some young men who were with him, renewed his threat that he was going to "cut their God damned hearts out." He wrested the poker from Mollie's hands and struck her with it before his pals intervened and escorted him away.

Shortly after the December incident, Andrews showed up at the Campbell house asking what sort of restitution he could make for the damage he had done. Mrs. Crawford told him that all she wanted was for him to stay away from her and her daughter, but Andrews kept coming back throughout early January, using "very insulting language" and otherwise pestering the Crawfords and the other female occupants of the Campbell house, before he was finally reported to the Springfield provost marshal's office and arrested on January 22.

Whatever mild punishment Andrews received for his antics at the Campbell house did not keep him from getting into trouble again two months later. On March 22, 1864, Andrews, who operated a saloon/grocery at the southeast corner of the square, was arrested for selling liquor to soldiers in violation of General Sanborn's special order. Among the witnesses against Andrews was James B. "Wild Bill" Hickok, employed by General Sanborn as a scout and spy in the Southwest District. Hickok swore that he had seen two soldiers drinking whiskey in Andrews's saloon on March 21. As in the disorderly conduct case, Andrews was again

James B. "Wild Bill" Hickok served in Springfield as a Union scout and spy during the latter part of the Civil War.

apparently let off with a light sentence, because he was still in the saloon business two months later when he paid the stipulated five-dollar tax levied by the government on the sale of intoxicating liquor.

Liquor violations like Andrews's sale of whiskey to soldiers were commonplace in Springfield during the Civil War, but in most instances the offenders were let off with a fine or other mild penalty. Persistent lawbreakers, however, were subject to having their supply of liquor confiscated or their businesses shut down. DeWitt Brewster and James H. Fagg, who ran a grocery store in the east part of Springfield, had their goods confiscated and their partnership broken up in the spring of 1864 for repeatedly selling liquor to soldiers, among other offenses. In March 1865, the assistant provost marshal ordered the Springfield firm of John A. Page closed and his stock of liquor confiscated for repeated offenses of selling liquor without a license dating back to the previous year.

Both civil and military police, of course, spent a disproportionate amount of time dealing with repeat offenders like Andrews and Page, whether the crime was a liquor violation or some other transgression. In May 1863, for example, a Springfield man named J. Fairchild was convicted in military court of passing counterfeit notes to pay gambling and other debts, and he was confined in Springfield. He escaped barely over a month later but apparently did not abscond from town (or else returned), as he was later charged with gambling in the spring of 1865.

Fairchild's escape was not unusual. The Springfield prisons were crowded with disloyalists and minor criminals, and security was lax. As early as March 1863, the *Springfield Journal* complained, "The escape of prisoners from the guard-house and prison in this place has become so common that it creates no surprise." The editorial criticism apparently did little to rectify the situation because less than two months later, forty-five prisoners escaped from the college prison on the same day.

Even as the war drew to a close, Springfield continued to witness an inordinate amount of petty crime. Although Springfield and its permanent residents had prospered to some extent in 1863 and 1864, the poverty and social chaos fostered by the Civil War in southwest Missouri had also given rise to a more or less permanent criminal class. The *Springfield Journal*'s assessment of the situation in January 1865 was only a slight exaggeration: "Never, to our recollection, has there been so much thieving and devilment carried on in our city as at the present time. It is becoming dangerous for a man to step out of his house after night, for fear of being shot by some drunken scamp, or 10 year old boy who is loaded with weapons."

Crimes committed by civilians in Springfield during the Civil War were handled by either the Greene County Court or the Union provost marshal, depending on who received the complaint and other circumstances of the case, while offenses by soldiers were handled exclusively by military authorities. In a few instances, Federal soldiers found guilty of desertion or a violent crime like murder were executed at Springfield. Perhaps the most notable military execution of the war, however, involved not a Federal soldier but a Confederate guerrilla named Charles Brownlee, who, during the early part of the war, had been involved in bushwhacking about one hundred miles north of Springfield in Moniteau and Cooper Counties. Brownlee was convicted in 1863 by military commission at Boonville of murder, robbery, and house burning and sentenced to be shot, but he escaped to Arkansas before the execution could be carried out, joined the regular Confederate army, and became a lieutenant. In the spring of 1865, as Brownlee was making his way north from Arkansas toward his home territory of Moniteau County, he was captured in Polk County and brought to Springfield. Despite his written appeal to General Sanborn, Brownlee was taken south of town on May 11 and shot in accordance with the verdict that had been pronounced on him two years earlier. Many Southern sympathizers criticized the execution as a "military murder," while Federal authorities denied that Brownlee was a Confederate officer.

On April 10, 1865, after word reached Springfield that General Robert E. Lee had surrendered to General Ulysses S. Grant at Appomattox, the soldiers and the Union citizens of Greene County gathered for a big celebration. A two-hundred-gun salute was fired from the forts, and according to Holcombe, orders were issued that any man found *sober* on the streets after 9:00 p.m. would be subject to a fine. Within a few days after Lee surrendered his army to Grant, other Confederate armies surrendered as well, and it was clear that an end to four agonizing years of civil war had finally come. Soldiers, both Federal and Confederate, gradually began returning to their Missouri homes, and the last Union troops marched out of Springfield in September 1865. It would be many years, however, before life for the soldiers or their loved ones would return to anything approaching normal.

Chapter 13

The Aftermath of the War

Although the Civil War officially ended in the spring of 1865, the rancor and discord it spawned persisted for many years and often gave rise to violence. Nowhere was this truer than the border state of Missouri, where political sentiment during the war had been so evenly and so adamantly split. As a predominantly Union area, Greene County was not as divided as certain other parts of Missouri, but bitterness left over from the war still shaped the political landscape in the Springfield vicinity for many years and directly or indirectly provoked a number of violent incidents.

The Missouri Constitution of 1865 that was adopted at the end of the Civil War only inflamed the lingering bitterness the war had produced. Usually called the Drake Constitution after Radical Republican Charles D. Drake, a prominent member of the constitutional convention and the document's chief architect, the new constitution provided that anyone who had ever been a member of the Confederate army or who had openly sympathized with the South could not vote, run for office, or hold certain jobs like preacher, teacher, or lawyer. The state convention passed the Drake Constitution in April 1865, and it was put to a vote of the people in June. Despite the fact that former Confederates were barred from voting on the document that would disenfranchise them, the new constitution passed statewide by only a narrow margin, although it passed overwhelmingly in Greene County. It went into effect on July 4, 1865.

One of the first events in Greene County in which the provisions of the Drake Constitution came into play was the trial of Wild Bill Hickok for killing Davis Tutt on the Springfield square on July 21, 1865. Although Hickok was a Federal scout and Tutt had been a Confederate soldier, political differences had nothing to do with the gunfight itself. However, when Hickok came to trial later in the summer, with John S. Phelps acting as his counsel and Pony Boyd serving as the judge, he was promptly found not guilty by reason of self-defense, despite the fact that the evidence indicated that Wild Bill had made no effort to avoid the showdown with Tutt and had even instigated it. Many of Tutt's friends and other observers cried foul, suggesting that the jury of Union men had been blinded by the loyalty issue, but their protests were to no avail.

The notorious reign of the Regulators, a vigilante group active in Greene County during the spring and summer of 1866, also had political overtones left over from the Civil War. The group, sometimes called the Honest Men's League, arose in response to an outbreak of horse thefts

Springfield square as it appeared near the time when the Regulators held a mass meeting there. Springfield, Missouri downtown, #00651, in the collection of Wilson's Creek National Battlefield. *Courtesy of National Park Service.*

and other crimes in northern Greene County that were thought to have been committed by ex-Confederate bushwhackers, and most of the men who joined the Regulators to combat the crime spree were strong Union men. Ironically, however, the first victim of the vigilante group was Green B. Phillips, the Enrolled Missouri Militia captain who had aided in the Federal defense at Fort No. 4 during the Battle of Springfield. Although Phillips was a Union man, at least in name, and was considered an upstanding citizen by most people, he had apparently befriended some of the suspected thieves, and he paid with his life for the indiscretion. The rule of the Regulators reached its zenith on May 28, 1866, when more than 250 of the self-appointed law enforcers galloped into Springfield on horseback and gathered on the square, where their leaders gave speeches proclaiming the law and order decrees of the Honest Men's League. Later the same day, south of Ozark, the vigilante mob overtook a fugitive from Greene County who had been charged with theft and strung him up on the spot to a big oak tree.

A few months later, a notorious incident, unrelated to the reign of the Regulators, that was a direct consequence of the Civil War and the Drake Constitution occurred just across the Greene County border in Webster County near present-day Elkland. Reverend Samuel S. Headlee, a circuit-riding minister and an unrepentant Confederate sympathizer, determined to preach at one of his old churches, Pleasant View, in defiance of the new constitution. Near the beginning of the Civil War, Headlee had knocked down a U.S. flag at the church, and the feeling against him ran high among the Radical Union men of the neighborhood. When Headlee showed up at the church on July 28, 1866, an armed mob was there to meet him and run him off. As he was leaving the premises, however, one of his tormentors, whose name ironically was Drake and who reportedly had been among the men who put up the flag five years earlier, overtook the preacher and filled him full of bullets. As Holcombe's history so aptly and wryly observed, "This was the way that brethren and followers of the meek and lowly Jesus dwelt together in unity in those days of the reconstruction period."

Citizens of Greene County also sought, in the latter part of the nineteenth century, to redress grievances left over from the Civil War in more mundane ways than trying to kill one another. They continued

Depiction of the murder of Reverend Samuel S. Headlee in the summer of 1866. *Drawing by Nic Frising.*

to sue one another for payment of debts or compensation for property destruction related to the war, just as they had begun doing while the conflict was yet raging. Nor were private individuals the only ones to seek recompense through the courts for alleged debts stemming from the war. As early as 1863, according to one report, Greene County itself undertook a lawsuit against the Federal government for rent and damages to the county courthouse during the Union occupation of Springfield. In 1907, forty-two years after the end of hostilities, the county presented another claim to the United States for use of the courthouse during the Civil War.

The First Christian Church of Springfield also filed several claims against the U.S. government, alleging that church property had been damaged or destroyed while the building was being used as a hospital and barracks during the war. The church was paid $160 for use of its building after the Battle of Wilson's Creek, but the suit for damages was disallowed at that time. A second suit resulted in another rent payment in 1874, but the damage claim was again disallowed. The First Christian Church, however, was nothing if not persistent, and the government finally authorized payment for the damage claim in 1907, although the question of whether the church ever received such payment is unclear.

The most objectionable provisions of the Drake Constitution were repealed in the early 1870s, and the power of the Radical Republicans gradually waned during the decade. At the same time, Missouri witnessed a resurgence of the Democratic Party, and General Marmaduke, who had led the Confederates at the Battle of Springfield, was even elected governor of the state in 1884. After an uncharacteristic period of political one-sidedness during the years of Radical Republican rule immediately after the Civil War, Missouri had regained its equilibrium, but considerations carried over from the war continued to shape political and social events in the Ozarks in one fashion or another well into the 1880s. For instance, the rise of the celebrated Bald Knobbers, a vigilante group that was active in Taney County in the early to mid-1880s, had its roots in the political divisions wrought by the Civil War. Most of the Bald Knobbers were ex–Union Republicans who were dissatisfied with what they saw as a lack of law and order in the county and a feeble determination on the part of Democratic county officials, many of whom were ex-Confederates, to do anything about it. Even today, it is not difficult to find people in Missouri and the Ozarks who still harbor strong feelings about the issues of the Civil War, and the state's legacy of evenly divided political opinion, engendered before and during the war, has persisted, election cycle after election cycle, for 150 years.

Chapter 14

Postwar Commemoration

Few, if any, structures that existed during the Civil War remain in Springfield. For instance, the courthouse that served as a hospital and prison during the war was torn down in 1914. The fields of battle during Zagonyi's charge and the Battle of Springfield are also beyond protection, having been engulfed by the town's growth during the late nineteenth century and early twentieth century. Thus, efforts to memorialize the actions that occurred on Springfield soil during the Civil War and to honor the people who participated in those actions have focused more on commemoration than preservation.

As early as August 1865, less than four months after the war ended and a month and a half before the last of the Federal soldiers stationed at Springfield would leave town, a meeting was held at the courthouse to discuss raising funds for erection of a Federal monument at the Wilson's Creek battlefield. Although nothing became of this initial effort, it showed that Greene Countians had a sense of obligation to remember the sacrifice of those who fought in the Civil War almost from the time the combatants laid down their weapons.

The National Cemetery was established at Springfield in 1867 on a five-acre tract of land near the present-day intersection of Glenstone and Seminole. Bodies of Federal soldiers from the Civil War who had been buried throughout southwest Missouri, including those in and about Springfield, were dug up and reinterred at the new cemetery, and an agent of the U.S. government came to Springfield to supervise the work.

The bodies of the Confederate dead remained neglected until late 1869, when an organization was formed at Springfield to attend to their reburial. Over the next few years, the group raised funds to purchase a four-acre tract of land adjoining the National Cemetery, and more than five hundred bodies of former Southern soldiers from in and around Springfield, nearly half of them from Wilson's Creek, were disinterred and reburied at the new cemetery. Very few of the graves were marked, since the identities of the remains were unknown.

Over the years, the National Cemetery has expanded and added monuments and other enhancements. On Decoration Day 1873, for example, the Bailey monument, which had been erected in accordance with the will of Springfieldian Dr. T.J. Bailey, was dedicated to the citizens

The Bailey Monument at the National Cemetery, dedicated to the citizens and soldiers who defended Springfield during the Battle of Springfield. *Photo by author.*

Monument to General Lyon, moved from the square to the National Cemetery in the mid-1880s. *Photo by author.*

Union veterans' reunion on the square in Springfield in 1883. Springfield reunion, square, #31378, in the collection of Wilson's Creek National Battlefield. *Courtesy of National Park Service.*

and soldiers who were killed in defense of the town during the Battle of Springfield. In 1874, the cemetery was enclosed by a limestone wall. A monument to General Lyon, erected on the public square and dedicated during a veterans' reunion in 1883, was moved the following year to the National Cemetery.

Additions were also made to the Confederate Cemetery after it was established in 1871. The ground expanded to include 6.3 acres, and a stone wall was erected around the 2.7 acres where the graves were located. In the mid-1880s, an effort to beautify the cemetery was undertaken, and headstones were placed on many of the graves. After the beautification effort, a dedication ceremony was held in 1887, at which time it was reported that "now the confederate cemetery will compare favorably in beauty with the federal cemetery adjoining." In

Monument to Sterling Price, erected at the Confederate Cemetery in 1901. *Photo by author.*

1901, a fifteen-foot monument honoring General Sterling Price was erected at the cemetery.

In 1911, the Confederate Cemetery was incorporated into the National Cemetery, and the unified cemetery has continued to see improvements and additions, including a 4.3-acre expansion to the west of the original cemetery. In 1958, the United Daughters of the Confederacy erected a monument in the Confederate portion of the cemetery to the numerous unknown Southern soldiers thought to be buried at or near the site. In 2003, the local camp of the Sons of Union Veterans placed a two-sided memorial at the cemetery to the Federal soldiers who were killed in the Springfield area or died in Springfield hospitals during the war.

Efforts to commemorate the Civil War in Springfield have not been confined just to the National Cemetery. In 1931, the University Club of Springfield erected a historical marker memorializing Major Zagonyi's celebrated charge, sometimes called the First Battle of Springfield. Originally placed at the old Frisco Station at the corner of Phelps and Main, it was later moved to West Mount Vernon Street, nearer the site where the action occurred. A city park on West Mount Vernon Street is also named in honor of Zagonyi, and another historical marker commemorating the charge of Fremont's Body Guard was placed there in 2008 by the Missouri Department of Natural Resources.

In 1963, the Greene County Historical Society placed a monument in Phelps Grove Park commemorating John S. Phelps and his homesite. In 2001, historical markers were placed by the Wilson's Creek National Battlefield Foundation and the City of Springfield at twelve points of interest pertaining to the Battle of Springfield. Forming a tour route, the markers are designed to be viewed in sequence. In 2005, an additional historic marker commemorating the overall Battle of Springfield was placed on the public square by the Missouri Department of Natural Resources (although it has been temporarily removed while renovation is taking place on the square). On September 30, 2011, the local tent of the Daughters of Union Veterans dedicated a historic marker on the grounds of Sunshine Elementary School to honor the work of Mary Whitney Phelps, who, at the close of the Civil War, founded a home in Springfield for orphans of soldiers killed during the war.

Historic marker in Zagonyi Park near the site of Zagonyi's celebrated charge. *Photo by author.*

One of twelve historic markers pertaining to the Battle of Springfield placed throughout the town in 2001. *Photo by author.*

When the Confederate Cemetery was incorporated into the National Cemetery in 1911, the deed stipulated that the Confederate portion of the unified cemetery would only be used for burials of men who had served the Confederate States of America. However, by the mid-twentieth century, a large part of the Confederate portion of the National Cemetery had still never been used, while the rest of the cemetery was running out of space. In negotiations with the Department of the Army, the Missouri Division of the United Daughters of the Confederacy (UDC) agreed to the unrestricted use of the 3.6 acres of the Confederate portion of the cemetery lying outside the stone wall. In 1948, the Confederate Cemetery Association, by deed, removed the restrictions on the 3.6 acres outside the wall that had been written into the 1911 deed, and in 1957 that portion of the old Confederate Cemetery was opened up for burial of veterans from any war. Even in the 2.7-acre enclosed portion of the old Confederate Cemetery, however, there remained many unoccupied grave sites that would never be used, and in 1981 the Confederate Cemetery Association of Missouri and the then Veterans Administration reached an agreement removing all restrictions on burials within the enclosed portion and allowing burials of all veterans there as well.

In 1984, the walled portion of the old Confederate Cemetery was opened for burial of veterans from any war, and a plaque was placed on the south side of the Sterling Price monument by the Veterans Administration. It was dedicated to the United Daughters of the Confederacy Missouri Division, in a ceremony held on August 10, the anniversary of the Battle of Wilson's Creek, to commemorate the integration of the cemetery. In the spirit of reconciliation shown by the UDC in taking steps to remove deed restrictions on 485 unoccupied Confederate sites in the Springfield National Cemetery so they would be available to all veterans and their dependents, and in the same spirit shown by the Veterans Administration in honoring those actions, it is perhaps fitting to close this book with a quote from the plaque. The efforts of the UDC, reads the tablet, "serve as a symbol of reunification of purpose for memorializing those who have honorably served this great nation without regard to past differences."

Bibliography

Books and Periodicals

Banasik, Michael E., ed. *Confederate "Tales of the War" in the Trans-Mississippi, Part One: 1861*. Iowa City, IA: Press of Camp Pope Bookshop, 2010.

———. *Duty, Honor and Country: The Civil War Experiences of Captain William P. Black, Thirty-seventh Illinois Infantry*. Iowa City, IA: Press of Camp Pope Bookshop, 2006.

———. *Missouri in 1861: The Civil War Letters of Franc B. Wilkie, Newspaper Correspondent*. Iowa City, IA: Camp Pope Bookshop, 2001.

Bearss, Edwin C., ed. *The Civil War Letters of Major William G. Thompson of the 20th Iowa Infantry Regiment*. Fayetteville, AR: Washington County Historical Society, 1966.

Bek, William G., trans. "The Civil War Diary of John T. Buegel, Union Soldier." Part I. *Missouri Historical Review* 40 (July 1946).

Black, Frances Carver, comp. *Marking Civil War History in the Ozarks: A Guide to Civil War Markers and Monuments in Twenty-four Southwest Missouri Counties*. Springfield, MO: Daughters of Union Veterans of the Civil War, Mary Whitney Phelps Tent, No. 22, 2010.

Dorsheimer, William. "Fremont's Hundred Days in Missouri." Parts II and III. *Atlantic Monthly* 9 (February and March, 1862).

Escott, George S. *History and Directory of Springfield and North Springfield*. Springfield, MO: Patriot-Advertiser, 1878.

Fairbanks, Jonathan, and Clyde Edwin Tuck. *Past and Present of Greene County, Missouri*. Indianapolis, IN: A.W. Bowen and Company, 1915.

Foley, James L. "With Fremont in Missouri, Part II." *Sketches of the War.* Edited by W.H. Chamberlin et. al. Cincinnati, OH: Robert Clarke Company, 1903.

Fremont, Jesse Benton. *The Story of the Guard: A Chronicle of the War*. Boston, MA: Ticknor and Fields, 1863.

Glazier, Robert C. "Historic Merger of Two Pioneer Presbyterian Churches to Be Celebrated in Observance of 75th Anniversary of Springfield's First and Calvary Presbyterian Church." *Springfield!* (October 2005).

Goman, Frederick W. *Up From Arkansas: Marmaduke's First Missouri Raid Including the Battles of Springfield and Hartville.* Springfield, MO: Wilson's Creek National Battlefield Foundation, 1999.

Holcombe, R.I., ed. *History of Greene County, Missouri*. Clinton, MO: The Printery, 1969. First published 1883.

Hubble, Martin J., ed. *Personal Reminiscences and Fragments of the Early History of Springfield Greene County, Missouri*. Springfield, MO: Inland Printing Company, 1914.

Huff, Leo E., ed. *The Civil War Letters of Albert Demuth and Roster Eighth Missouri Volunteer Cavalry*. Springfield, MO: Greene County Historical Society, 1997.

Ingenthron, Elmo. *Borderland Rebellion: A History of the Civil War on the Missouri-Arkansas Border*. Branson, MO: Ozarks Mountaineer, 1980.

Knox, Thomas W. *Camp-Fire and Cotton-Field: Southern Adventure in Time of War*. New York: Blelock and Company, 1865.

L'Aloge, Bob. *The Maiden Waved a Snowy Scarf: The Story of Springfield, Missouri, During the Civil War*. Sunnyside, WA: BJS Brand Books, 1993.

Lobdell, Jared C., ed. "The Civil War Journal and Letters of Colonel John Van Deusen Du Bois, April 12, 1861 to October 16, 1862." Part I. *Missouri Historical Review* 60, no. 4 (July 1966).

———. "The Civil War Journal and Letters of Colonel John Van Deusen Du Bois, April 12, 1861 to October 16, 1862." Part II. *Missouri Historical Review* 61, no. 1 (October 1966).

Meyer, Craig, ed. *Confederate Girlhoods: A Women's History of Early Springfield, Missouri*. Springfield, MO: Moon City Press, 2010.

Moore, Frank, ed. *The Rebellion Record: A Diary of American Events*. Vol. III. New York: G.P. Putnam, 1862.

Musser, Richard H. "The War in Missouri: From Springfield to Neosho." *Southern Bivouac* 4 (April 1886).

Neumann, Robert. *An Illustrated History of the Civil War in Springfield, Mo. 1861–1865*. Springfield, MO: self-published, 1975.

Patrick, Jeff, ed. *Nine Months in the Infantry Service: The Civil War Journal of R.P. Matthews and Roster the Phelps Regiment Missouri Volunteers*. Springfield, MO: Greene County Historical Society, 1999.

Piston, William G. "'Springfield Is a Vast Hospital': The Dead and Wounded at the Battle of Wilson's Creek." *Missouri Historical Review* 93, no. 4 (July 1999).

Piston, William G., and Richard W. Hatcher III. *Wilson's Creek: The Second Battle of the Civil War and the Men Who Fought It*. Chapel Hill: University of North Carolina Press, 2000.

Shephard, Edward M. "Early Springfield." *Missouri Historical Review* 24, no. 1 (October 1929).

Speer, William S., ed. *Encyclopedia of the New West*. Marshall, TX: United States Biographical Publishing Company, 1881.

Tilley, Nannie M., ed. *Federals on the Frontier: The Diary of Benjamin F. McIntyre 1862–1864*. Austin: University of Texas Press, 1963.

Vaught, Elsa, ed. *The Diary of an Unknown Soldier*. Van Buren, AR: Press-Argus Company, 1959.

War of the Rebellion: A Compilation of Official Records of the Union and Confederate Armies. 1880–1902. Reprint, CD-ROM. Oakman, AL: H-Bar Enterprises, 1996.

Ware, Eugene Fitch. *The Lyon Campaign in Missouri: Being a History of the First Iowa Infantry*. Topeka, KS: Crane and Company, 1907.

Wyatt, John. "A Confederate Diary." Part I. *White River Valley Historical Quarterly* 36, no. 2 (Fall 1996).

———. "A Confederate Diary." Part II. *White River Valley Historical Quarterly* 36, no. 3 (Winter 1997).

UNPUBLISHED MANUSCRIPTS AND DOCUMENTS

Anderson, Thomas L. Papers (C0678). State Historical Society of Missouri Manuscript Collection, Columbia.

Ash, David. Letters. U.S. Army Military History Institute, Carlisle, Pennsylvania.

Bennett, Lyman Gibson. Diary. Western Historical Manuscript Collection, Rolla. Online at Community and Conflict: The Impact of the Civil War in the Ozarks. www.ozarkscivilwar.org.

Bradbury, John F., Jr. *Fort No. 5: A Civil War Field Fortification in Springfield, Greene County, Missouri*. Prepared for the City of Springfield, 1984.

Branson, William W. Diary, 1861–62 (C0218). State Historical Society of Missouri Manuscript Collection, Columbia.

Donnell, Lemuel. Diary, 1861–65. Shiloh Museum of Ozark History, Springdale, Arkansas. Online at www.ozarkscivilwar.org.

Durbin-Dodd, Janice. *"O It Is Distressing Times Here in Missouri": The Impact of the Civil War on Civilians in Southwest Missouri*. Republic, MO: Wilson's Creek National Battlefield, 1995.

Flanagin, Harris. Flanagin Papers. Arkansas History Commission, Little Rock.

Fourth Military District Enrolled Missouri Militia Order Book, November 1862–May 1863 (C1099). State Historical Society of Missouri Manuscript Collection, Columbia.

Henry to Dear Sister. Letter, 12 August 1861. History Museum for Springfield–Greene County.

Kelso, Margaret Gilmore. *A True Story of My Life in the Ozarks and Memories of Civil War*. Kelso Family File, Springfield–Greene County Library.

MacDonald, Emmett. Order Book, 1862–63, MacDonald's Battery Flying Artillery (C2654). State Historical Society of Missouri Manuscript Collection, Columbia.

Rountree, William. Autobiography, circa 1932. Rountree Collection, History Museum for Springfield–Greene County. Online at www.ozarkscivilwar.org.

Springfield, Missouri History, Civil War. Information file, Springfield–Greene County Library.

U.S. Census records.

U.S. Provost Marshals Papers, Individual Citizens File. Microfilm copies at Missouri State Archives, Jefferson City.

U.S. Provost Marshals Papers, Two or More Citizens File. Microfilm copies at Missouri State Archives, Jefferson City.

Van Winkle, W.A. *A Report on Civil War Fortifications in Springfield, Missouri: Fort No. 1, Also Called Fort Brown, and Fort No. 2*. Presented to the Historical Site Board, Springfield, Missouri, July 1970.

Voelkner, Henry. Letters, 1861–62 (C0436). State Historical Society of Missouri Manuscript Collection, Columbia.

Wilkes, P.S. to J.F. Snyder. Letter, Dr. John F. Snyder Collection, Missouri Historical Society. Copy at History Museum for Springfield–Greene County.

Williams, O.A., to John Willsen. Letter, n.d. History Museum of Springfield–Greene County.

Newspapers

Bloomington (IL) Pantagraph.
Columbia Missouri Statesman.
Dubuque (IA) Weekly Times.
Emporia (KS) News.
Jefferson City Inquirer.
Kansas City Daily Western Journal of Commerce.
Lawrence (KS) Weekly Republican.
Liberty (MO) Tribune.

Little Rock Arkansas True Democrat.
Muscatine (IA) Weekly Journal.
New York Times.
Olathe (KS) Mirror.
Richmond (MO) Northwest Conservator.
Springfield Advertiser.
Springfield Equal Rights Gazette.
Springfield Journal.
Springfield Mirror.
St. Louis Daily Missouri Republican.
St. Louis Tri-Weekly Missouri Republican.
White Cloud Kansas Chief.

Index

L

M

N

O

P

Q

R

S

About the Author

Larry Wood is a retired public school teacher and a freelance writer. His historical articles have appeared in numerous publications, including *America's Civil War*, *Blue and Gray* magazine, *Missouri Life*, *Missouri Historical Review*, the *Ozarks Mountaineer*, *True West* and *Wild West*. Among his previous books are *The Two Civil War Battles of Newtonia* and *Wicked Joplin*. A native of Fair Grove, Wood received his BA and MA degrees from Missouri State University and now lives in Joplin with his wife, Gigi.

Also by Larry Wood:

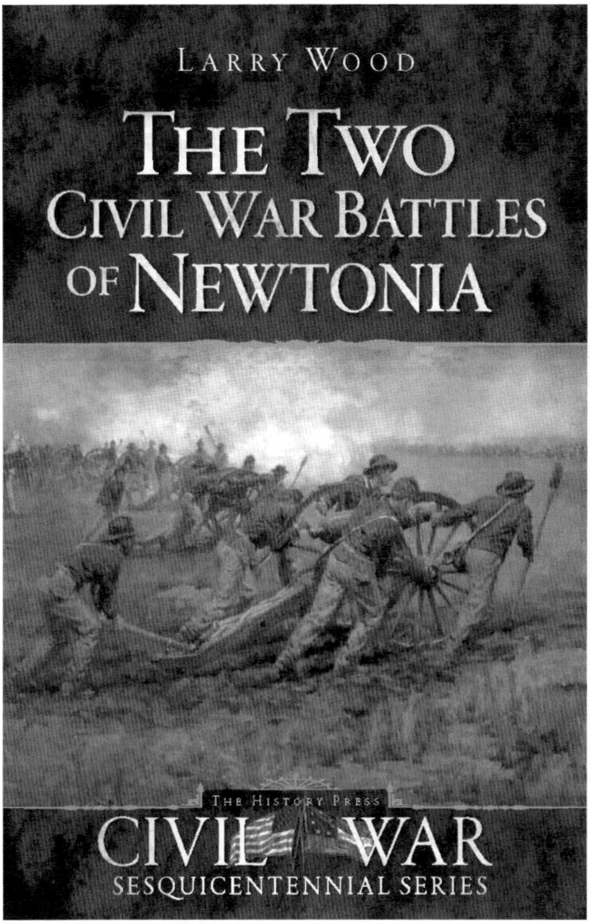

978.1.60949.857.6 * 6 x 9 * 160 pp * over 40 images * $19.99
The History Press | June 2010

Winner of the 2011 Walter Williams Major Work Award
from the Missouri Writer's Guild

The Two Civil War Battles of Newtonia:
Fierce and Furious